how to be loved

how to be loved

A Memoir of Lifesaving Friendship

≈

EVA HAGBERG FISHER

Houghton Mifflin Harcourt
Boston · New York
2019

hmhco.com

Library of Congress Cataloging-in-Publication Data
Names: Hagberg, Eva, author.
Title: How to be loved : a memoir of lifesaving friendship / Eva Hagberg Fisher.
Description: Boston : Houghton Mifflin Harcourt, 2019.
Identifiers: LCCN 2018006363 (print) | LCCN 2018007599 (ebook) |
ISBN 9780544991163 (ebook) | ISBN 9780544991156 (hardback)
Subjects: LCSH: Hagberg, Eva. | Mast cell disease—Patients—United
States—Biography. | Cancer—Patients—United States—Biography. |
Friendship—United States—Case studies. | BISAC: BIOGRAPHY &
AUTOBIOGRAPHY / Personal Memoirs. | FAMILY &
RELATIONSHIPS / Friendship. |
BIOGRAPHY & AUTOBIOGRAPHY / Medical. |
BIOGRAPHY & AUTOBIOGRAPHY / Women.
Classification: LCC RC924.5.M37 (ebook) | LCC RC924.5.M37 H34 2019 (print) |
DDC 616.7/70092—dc23
LC record available at https://lccn.loc.gov/2018006363

Book design by Emily Snyder

Printed in the United States of America
DOC 10 9 8 7 6 5 4 3 2 1

To Melanie

act one

one

~

When Allison and I met, it was not love at first sight. Or second, or third, or even ninth. For the first year that we knew each other, all I could see was that she was different from me. I was almost thirty, and well. She was nearly sixty, and sick. She was dying and I would never die (so I believed, so we all believe, until we can't anymore, until we never will anymore).

I would never have met Allison if I weren't used to going to rooms filled with sober alcoholics who talked to each other in a concerted effort to stay that way. When I moved from New York City to Berkeley for graduate school in the fall of 2010, I looked for the closest alcoholics-filled room to campus, and got ready to make myself a new home. And the first day I walked into the particular room in which Allison and I met, I saw the same configuration that I would see almost every day for the next eight years — wooden chairs lining the walls, wooden slats lining the windows and letting the sun beam in, a metaphor for all of us who had been so used to the darkness of alcoholism that the sun was warming us, burning off our histories as philanderers and thieves and liars. And I did what I usually did in social situations, which was to scan and assess: looking first for a boy I could get into some trouble with and then a girl I could maybe also get into some trouble with, and then for who seemed to be in charge, and who wasn't, and in my scanning, and in my assessment of possible power and possible sexual gratification and possible friendship with someone who would help me be cool and/or elusively popular, I didn't really notice the woman who sat by the door, focused almost entirely on her tiny brown and white dog.

The woman who, once I did notice her, looked like she was in her late fifties or early sixties or maybe late forties. The woman who had dark hair that fell around her face like a lopsided crown, and who had a face unlike any I had ever seen before. Her mouth was small and her cheeks big, her jaw line ill-defined, her neck padded with pockets of fat—were those jowls? But she wasn't fat, it wasn't that; it just seemed that her body had been somehow rearranged. Her arms were thin and her trunk compensated, and she wore shoes with low heels, and, as I would come to see over days and then months and then years, always jeans and a button-down shirt and a sweatshirt and a jacket, and she always wore Sadie's leash like it was another piece of clothing. Later, when she was dying, I would borrow her sweatshirts and her jackets to take Sadie for walks when Allison was too tired to take her out herself, and I would find little free-floating chicken bits that she kept loose in her pockets to feed to Sadie every time the dog behaved herself by sitting quietly and unobtrusively in the meeting, every time Sadie didn't totally freak out when people clapped, as they invariably did, when someone announced that they had just reached thirty days or thirty years or some milestone of a day in between.

A group of us with an hour to spare between the end of the meeting and the start of classes on the campus across the street used to get lunch together at an outside food court a block away. I started joining, tentatively, hanging back, focusing on my burrito, my pad thai, still trying to figure out where the ladder was and where I might belong. Whenever Allison spoke, it was clear she ran the place. It was confusing to me because she was also the most open, the quickest to admit she didn't know what to do. I'd never seen someone show that much of her soft belly and receive that much respect. I wanted to connect with her, but I couldn't figure out my angle of approach. Were we equals about to bond? Was she the alpha and I the beta? Vice versa? Was I smarter than her? Was she smarter than me? I'd often thought of making friends akin to the process of landing a plane: assess the runway, consider the angle and speed of approach, then go. Hope it isn't too bumpy. Brake, but not too quickly. But with Allison, all those calculations just didn't work.

The first time we finally spoke to each other, her barreling through my performance of quiet listening (a cover-up for the frenzy of social math going on in my head), was on one of these lunches, in September, when I was still new to everything: this meeting, graduate school, the city, the state. The usual stuff — resentments, fears, the daily attempts not to drink in the face of life circumstances that had us virtually destroyed — had come up during the meeting itself; lunch was where we went to bond, to recap, to recast our stories in a kinder and softer light. What was spoken of in the meeting in terms of darkness and pain and fear was laughed about over our lunches afterward, and no one laughed more compassionately than Allison.

"What classes are you taking?" she asked me. She told me she was auditing an English department lecture. Shakespeare.

"Architectural history, art history, another one about . . . cities," I said. I was trying to edit for her, stay away from academic terms that might be, I thought, beyond the scope of her interest—or understanding.

"And how's it going?"

I dissembled. I told her that it was fine, of course. I was having a hard time with the reading, sometimes, but it was good. Really good! I was learning and being challenged and this was nothing like New York but I could do it. The truth is that I was drowning, that I was starting to believe that I wasn't good enough to do this. That I was smart, but not smart enough for this.

"Have you made good friends in your program?"

A pause. I didn't feel like I'd come to grad school to make friends. My cohorts were my competition. Or they were people I could maybe sleep with. Or people who could help me get ahead. But I didn't think *friendship* was going to be a central part of my grad school experience. Accomplishment was.

"Are you finding the other students helpful?"

Wait, what? My colleagues and I sort of helped each other, but most of us were also in battle for coveted slots in the PhD program, to which we hadn't yet been admitted, and for which we would have the chance to formally apply at the end of our first year (with the implicit understanding that the interview had begun the day we arrived on campus). I was floating around in master's student purgatory, focusing on that degree but also, every day, waiting and wondering if this could be the day I would make a good enough impression to be eventually let in, let up the next rung of the academic ladder, recommended to continue. It's no wonder I was so insecure; every time I spoke in seminar I wondered if this would be a strike for or against me, if what I'd said would be a notch in my favor or a reason to let me go. I felt like there was something wrong with me for feeling so tied to the inscrutable opinions of my professors, and I felt ashamed at how deeply seated my anxieties about performance seemed to be, the ways in which I went over and over sentences after I'd said them, convinced I'd made some intractably inane observation about train lines, or Marx, or the midcentury American brutalist architect Paul Rudolph, sure that this time I had confirmed that I would be encouraged to *pursue an alternative career,* as academic rejection tended to be framed. Allison must have sensed all of this in the way I answered her, because she started talking about herself—a trick I later saw her do with everyone she spoke to, a way of relating to the basic feelings, no matter the details.

"Insecurity's a tough one," she said. "And it's hard to live the way we do."

I asked her what she meant, politely trying to engage her.

"What we do here, admitting that we're broken," she clarified. But *I* wasn't broken. I was fixable.

"Well, I'm broken," she said. "And you're broken. Of course you're broken. That's why you're here!"

She might have meant within the community that went to the meeting, or she might have meant graduate school itself.

"I dunno about that," I said. "I just have to stop worrying so much . . . and trust it will get better." What I meant was that *I* would get better.

"Well . . . the thing is, I'm not here to fix myself," she said. She never told me I was wrong, just offered her own alternative.

"For *me,* I just want comfort. I want to go where it's warm."

I had believed all along the way that I wasn't broken, just bruised. That the path that I was undertaking — the inventories, the amends, the relentless focus on honesty and truth and acting well even if I didn't feel well — was, at its core, an extensive self-improvement project.

As I listened to her talk, I felt myself detach from her, took an internal step back.

I'd had a real guide in New York, not this kind of comfort-seeking love stuff. I'd worked with a tough woman who'd pushed me to open doors for others, make apologetic phone calls when I'd screwed up, read her a list of every single person I'd ever resented (there were many). It didn't sound like Allison had been wrung out that way. It sounded like she had gotten here and people had loved her and she had loved them and that was it. I believed I was on this path so that I could stop being selfish or fragile or insecure. So that I could stop going home with people I shouldn't be going home with. So that I could get over my childhood and move forward, and up, ever upward. So that I could justify everything I had ever done, could write off my moral experiments, could *fix* myself. I was in a process of trying to dig out my insides and remake myself according to this new hand-book, because I'd never felt like I'd been given one, and I was into this idea that I was just bruised, just needed a little reorganization, and then I would be different. Better. Alli-son, meanwhile, seemed to be coming around and hanging out for some collective countercultural group bonding, for deep and accepting friendship.

She kept talking, pausing to take tiny bites of chicken and broccoli stir-fry, no ginger. She hated ginger ever since the first chemo; little bits of information like that kept cropping up and into our conversations. I heard words like "commu-nity" and "sitting together" and "acceptance" and "joy" and I also heard "chemo suite" and "steroids" and "trial failure" and this was an alternative universe, one where community was more than an abstraction, and also one where treatment had a location, a side drug, a failure rate. The campanile bell rang twice. Those of us with classes to get to picked up our backpacks, made motions to leave. Empty plates were put on the carryout trays; half-full plates left on top of trash cans for the men and women who lived in nearby People's Park and sometimes came through in search of the students' leftovers. Allison could tell we were all leaving and that she needed to wrap up. Still she compelled our attention, even as we were half standing, half sitting, heads leaning down to hear her, eyes fixed on her face. "The way I see it, I have two holes in my head," she said. "There's one on the top, where all the wisdom pours in, and then I have this other hole in my neck, and so I hear everything, and it's in my brain for a minute, maybe a day, and then . . . it's gone." The solution, she told us, was to keep listening, to keep her head open so that more wisdom could keep being poured in, so that even as it disappeared almost as soon as it had entered her head, there was enough so that, over time, it saturated her brain.

~

Later, when I came to her with a hole drilled into my head, with a skull that had been saturated in hydrogen peroxide, missing a piece of my brain that I had lost to a surgeon's hand, we laughed and laughed and laughed.

~

But when she said it, I couldn't understand what she meant. I was used to everything flowing into my brain and staying there. I had developed a dilettantish ability to know just enough about basically everything that I could participate in pretty much any dinner party conversation — just up until the point of actual engagement with the idea at hand. I had zero depth of knowledge, had no sense of a "field of expertise" beyond early twenty-first-century New York City architecture, which had been my professional beat for six years, but I did feel confident that once I heard something I didn't forget it. I could remember where on a page a sentence had appeared, could remember that Roland Barthes wrote "From Work to Text" while Michel Foucault wrote *What Is an Author?,* even though both essentially argued the same thing: that the written words are not what matter so much; that the text is created by the relationship between reader and words, that it is fluid and ever-changing and dependent on the whims and histories of whoever's absorbing it. Of course I'd be able to remember everything that everyone said. I certainly didn't have a hole in my neck where all the wisdom poured out.

~

The months went on and I went to my seminars and wrote my papers and fought every day the insecurity that came with not fully understanding words like *doxa* and *discipline,* and so I kept coming to the room and I kept hearing Allison, still talking about love, about acceptance, about missing her husband, who had died five years earlier (why wasn't she over it, I wondered, it had been *five years*) and still I had impostor syndrome and still I hadn't found my people and still I was wary of her, couldn't figure out her game. But I did pick up over time that she shouldn't be alive, shouldn't have been alive for the last six years. That her references to chemo suites and steroid nights came from a breast cancer ten years earlier that had gone into remission, then reappeared, in her liver. That six years earlier she had been given six months to live, but here she was, somehow still existing, under constant oncological supervision and near-constant treatment, various chemotherapies and proto-chemotherapies and radiation treatments and ablations and surgeries. I found all of this impressive and fantastical, but it also slotted her into a category of person I had no interest in (was afraid of): the sick.

I lived in somewhat peaceful but mostly wary coexistence with Allison (who told me later that she had found me abrasive, self-centered, impossible to crack) while I tried to find my crew. In college, I'd been in the center of a group of brilliant writers and poets and filmmakers and artists and musicians, but I'd always *felt* that I was on the periphery, that I was missing something, that I'd come in too late and was the perpetual new addition, that I was catching up the best I could but hadn't learned the rules. I'd stayed as close as I could to some of these friends once we all moved to New York, but once we were finding our ways in young adulthood I began to contend with separation via alcoholism and separation via ambition and separation via fear. In New York, I'd grown to be part of a design-publishing crowd, and my new friends had also been my editors, or my colleagues, or the editors of my colleagues. And I told myself that because my friends were also my professional acquaintances and — because I was a freelancer — in some way potentially responsible for my financial stability, of course I couldn't and shouldn't open up to them. I see now that I wouldn't have known how to even if I had wanted to, but because there was this extra layer of power embedded — they were editors who could give me work; or designers who could give me access — I was careful to try to keep my emotional distance. I spent hours and hours and hours with these people, and their approach was not mine, their story is not mine. Their friendships with each other, I saw later, I see today, were deep and intimate and honest and true — still are. It was my own fear, my own sense of distance, one learned from the moment I could speak and read, that kept me from the kinds of bonds that I saw them forge with each other, off the screen of our wild nights out. But that was like deep space for me: inaccessible, unmappable, completely remote.

I wanted the comfort of a power structure in Berkeley, so I turned first to the professors. I wanted to be the favorite, coddled, told I'd be a star. I had dreams of being hired immediately after graduation, of being the first to finish my PhD. Stepping into the architectural history graduate student workroom, I met my cohort, and looked to place myself on the ladder—smarter than the social historian over here; not as smart as the nineteenth-century-focused theorist over here. Right from the start, I was imbalanced, unequal, already separate, looking for people to tell me how great I was for having already published, for being a professional returning to school. I starved for the idea that I might know where I fit on the ladder, that I could be better. There had always been safety in being better, never safety in being equal.

Now, now that I know how destructive this separation is, how much my setting myself apart from people prevented me from ever feeling truly a part of anything, of anyone's life or journey or story or self, I wish I could go back and pay more attention to and be more open with my college friends, my New York friends, my colleagues, the people with whom I was in the trenches of graduate school. But back then, my alternative was still safer. I didn't need to change—not yet.

∾

By the time I met Allison, then, I'd never felt truly close to someone, not the way I'd seen other people be close to their friends; had never shown all of my selves, the most private and intimate and deepest selves, not to anyone. I had connections, friendships, some of which had lasted more than a decade, but there was always some distancing. I'd show one friend the side of me that was grieving over a relationship; another friend the side of me that believed, down to my core, that love was possible. But to show both sides to one person? Impossible. And so I compartmentalized. Categorized. Found moments of truth in drugs and alcohol but never in clarity, never in moments that lasted. I lied by omission. I swerved. That isn't how I wanted to be, but it was all that I knew. And when I met someone new, instead of listening, or being open, I judged. I'd been taught that by the rubrics of my family, which focused on achievement, production, the presentation of perfect self in everyday life, to misquote the social theorist Erving Goffman. Later, of course, as I unwound over the course of four years of constant and life-threatening illness, I would understand why my behavior could have seemed sociopathic, as it was sometimes called, why I had created that distance. But before Allison loved me into becoming a different person, until, as I told her before she died, she midwifed the person I had wanted to be into existence, I couldn't get what all the fuss was about.

And then, finally, things started to change. Not because of me, but because of her.

An early evening in November, I was walking down College Avenue toward the Rockridge BART station. I had my headphones in, because I always had my headphones in, because otherwise the chatter in my head, the noise that told me that I was assessing things incorrectly, that I shouldn't have said that thing to that professor, that my attempts at my life changes were totally failing, became deafening, but even above the music I heard a

"Hey! Eva!"

And to my left I saw a green Honda, a car I would later drive to the hospital to take her to the oncologist who would tell her she was really dying this time; a make and model of car I would years later see, sometimes, on the streets of Berkeley and look for her and forget that she was dead, but for now it was just Allison, alive, with Sadie on a blanket in the front seat.

"Get in!"

I got in, putting Sadie on my lap, but not before putting on the social armature of *dealing with an old and sick person.* I prepared to be polite, respectful. I prepared myself for talking about general topics—books, grad school, perhaps some gossip from the meeting. I prepared myself to have a social interaction that would just slip its way into my roster of social interactions that I needed to get through to get to the next thing. And instead, I looked at her and saw her face and her eyes and her tiny mouth from which so many words had poured, and from which a few more came, and a tightness in my chest uncoiled, just a millimeter.

"Where are you headed?"

I wanted to lie, to dissemble the same way I'd dissembled the specifics of school, but instead, as I felt that tightness uncoil just another millimeter, I edged into addressing reality.

"A party, in the city, with this guy—it's his birthday."

And then, truth:

"I'm worried I'm going to sleep with him."

"Is that likely?"

I told Allison how I'd met Matt. Two years earlier, in the airport in line for a delayed flight headed from New York to Heathrow, where we'd started talking and then exchanged emails and then decided to hang out in London. How we'd had a mini fling, which was relevant because I was in the middle of switching from one relationship to another, adding a third person to the mix because—

"Of course you did," she interrupted. I continued on, saying I wanted to —

"Feel alive!" she interrupted again.

"I've always seen him in cities neither of us lives in, and it's weird now that we live in the same place," I said.

I was also, because of my interest in recovery as self-improvement, trying not to just randomly fuck people. I wanted to change things up, have a good relationship maybe, or at least stop what wasn't working for me anymore. Sleeping with Matt would be a total backslide — it didn't fit into the story I was building, the bettering-of-self I was aiming for. "This is going backwards, and, I mean, it's bad behavior, right?"

Now was the time for her to say something wise and also in line with my original thought. I waited for her to tell me to live my best life now and not give my precious gift away. Or to tell me that having sex with someone I wasn't dating *was* bad behavior, was something I should stop doing. Everyone else in my life was advising me to change my ways. I was sober and yet I had this predilection for going to bars and sipping club soda while everyone else got hammered, and then finding a target and casually flirting and then bringing him home, and the last person I'd done this with had had a girlfriend — whom I'd met, ten minutes before I took him home. "I have a hall pass," he'd told me, and I hadn't cared that he was probably lying. Because my wants were more important than the truth.

"The thing is, it doesn't matter if you fuck him or not: you're still you," she said. "We are not saints."

Sure, we weren't saints, but we were always trying to improve, right? I had thought everything we were doing in the meetings we went to was about Becoming a Better Person and Developing Better Habits, and here, in this car in the rain, Allison had just offered me something different.

And then it was seven thirty and I had to leave, had to make it to the group dinner at the hot new restaurant, and so I reached across the car to do what I'd always seen everyone do with Allison—touch her, hold her, squeeze her shoulder and her arm. I didn't do it because I wanted connection, but because it felt like the next right thing to do to maintain kindness, to acknowledge her. I'd seen people touch her like that in meetings, and would learn later about the particular physical tourism of illness, the way in which we begin to sanctify those who are closer to death than we believe we are. Later, I would be touched in the way that she was; touristed in the way she was. But that was later, after I got sick, after I joined her kingdom.

~

"Heyyyy, how'd it go?" she asked the next day when I dragged myself into the room. I was mortified to report that, after all that, I hadn't even had the opportunity not to sleep with him. I'd shown up and he'd been happy to see me and then he'd introduced me to a girl, and I had realized that he was probably dating that girl, and I had felt the storms of ten thousand rejections, and instead of trying to navigate the difference and the distance between what I wanted and what I believed I wanted and what I felt I should want, I had focused on her, befriended her, chatted with her for an hour about work and my publications and this and that and graduate school and nothing real, because if someone saw something real, I might die. But I couldn't tell Allison that. I couldn't translate my experience of feeling rejected and broken into something true, and so instead —

"Oh, it was good," I said. "Thank you for your help."

And then I avoided her. Because the way she had seen my humanity, and the way she had accepted it, was loosening that tightness in my chest, uncoiling it, but too quickly. I wasn't ready for that yet. And besides, she'd lived this long, of course she'd keep surviving; I had all the time in the world with her.

~

But then, just like that, a few months later, her cancer returned. She needed more chemo, something stronger than the Herceptin she'd been semi-regularly infused with to help keep her breast cancer at bay. She said this cancer was probably in her liver again, although I couldn't understand how she had breast cancer in her liver — wouldn't that be liver cancer? — and I had so much to learn about medicine and doctors and cytotoxic drugs and steroids and metastasis and love.

But her cancer came back and I felt that I should *do something* because that's what everyone else around me seemed to be doing — extra hugs and sideways head tilts and the look that said at once "I pity you and I am afraid of you," and I would watch myself looking at her body — her thin arms and her huge butt — and I would wonder where the cancer was and where the chemo was and how she was being treated and also how it felt to be in her body. Did cancer hurt? And I wondered why she wasn't used to it — why it seemed like this was such a big deal for her. I'd heard her talk about chemo and surgeries and radiations, and most of all her fear of CT scans, her nervous anxiety that made her talk for longer than the four minutes we informally allotted each person, and I didn't understand how she wasn't used to it by now. *I* was used to it—to her having cancer. And I couldn't imagine, couldn't fathom, a life that was lived between scans, where each prospect of that whirring tube was more terrifying than the last. (Until I joined her.)

I didn't yet know how to be with her in a meaningful way, but I knew that I could bring food, enjoyed feeling like I was being of service, and useful, could proudly report to my spiritual guide that I had done a good deed that week, and so one Friday night I offered to bring Allison dinner from the Whole Foods near her house, and she accepted, gratefully, and I arrived, and we sat down at her kitchen table and she told me about her cancer, about where it was, and I said things like "I can't imagine" as I slowly shook my head in the performance of baffled confusion in the face of a kind person's illness that I'd seen others do.

"It's everywhere in my liver," she said, holding and stroking her right side with her right hand as with the other hand she took a bite of roast chicken, of the broccoli she loved. I didn't even know the liver was on the right side. I didn't know how badly cancer could hurt.

"TV on the bed?" she asked, as I cleared her plate and threw out my paper box of macaroni and cheese.

I'd only ever gotten in bed with someone I'd been having sex with. I thought of the artist Tracey Emin's tent, embroidered with the names of, as it was titled, *Everyone I Have Ever Slept With,* and how I'd seen it in London during the

Sensation show in 1999, and how I'd assumed, of course, that everyone listed would be someone she'd had sex with, but her mother was on there, her friends. I'd never been in bed with someone, been so intimate with someone that I wasn't trying to sleep with, and the categories, now that we were about to get in bed together, confused me. I couldn't figure out where to slot Allison — was she a sick old woman I was helping? Was she a sick wise sage who was helping me? Was she someone I was going to have sex with?

I helped her up and we walked into the bedroom, its bed pushed to the corner, a huge TV on the wall, and every surface — the long desk, two chairs, the bookshelves, the top of the bookshelves — covered in stacks of books. Strout, the Ann/es (Patchett and Tyler), Lively, Colwin. Everything she read had the same strand of inquiry, the same question. How should we live? And the room smelled, of laundry, which she did every day, but also of a faint but bright acidity, a smell I categorized as belonging to her specifically until I smelled it again, years later, in an oncology suite bathroom, and almost fell to the floor from recognition and grief.

We decided to watch *Crazy, Stupid, Love,* figured out how to get the Roku to get us there, and soon were watching a scene of Ryan Gosling's character trying to give Steve Carell's the best pickup tricks.

"God, I feel for you girls now," Allison said. "We didn't have to play all these games."

I looked over at her. She pressed pause and turned to me.

"I just loved William and fucked him all the time," she said. William was her dead husband. "It was sex! It wasn't so *complicated.*"

I didn't know what to say. It did seem that complicated

to me. Sex required games, diffusion, performance. I picked up my phone, pretended I needed to send a text.

(How many hours, I wonder now, did I miss with her because of my phone, because of needing to send a text?)

She pressed play. And then, I reached for a cookie from the bag we had brought in and placed at the foot of the bed, and lost my balance, and grabbed on to her arm, lightly, for stability. But instead of letting go, I gave her a squeeze, the briefest rub, just to acknowledge the touch, to finish it delicately instead of abruptly.

"That feels so good," she said.

I forced myself to pause. To open my palm, to lay it against her arm. The tightness inside me unwound again, just one more millimeter. She shifted, sitting up so that her entire upper back was pulled away from the wall. She was wearing a gray cashmere cardigan and I tentatively touched her upper back. I felt her soften under my touch, felt her settle in to what felt for her like an easy intimacy — something I had never experienced. I hadn't been held much as a child, hadn't automatically learned to hug and squeeze and pat and touch, and so Allison's ease with touch, with responding to touch, with asking for it, was new to me.

"Oh, that's so nice," she said as I moved my hand across her shoulders, as I flattened my hand and spread my fingers and made even more space for contact. The comfort she felt with herself and her own body, even as her body was racked with a pain she could barely describe even in poetry, was as foreign to me as the London hotel room in which I'd been in bed with Matt.

As I touched her body I felt how acutely I had lost any sense of mine. I could not have known if something felt good. I lived in my body knowing that it was the vessel for my mind, but beyond that it was irrelevant. And so Allison's desire for touch confused me, required a certain level of purposeful accommodation, of almost tangible effort. And yet the way in which she invited me to touch her was also a way of her touching me. This was not one-way, not a pat or a stroke of the arm, not the forced hugs I'd seen her experience at the end of the meetings. My hand was touching her, but her back was touching me. We were in this together.

When I think about Allison now, I feel the softness of her cashmere sweater under my hand, can sense the vastness of its gray color everywhere in my perception field. Years after we watched the movie, and weeks before she died, as I was trying to tell her who she had been to me, the words that came to mind were "second mother," but she wasn't that — our relationship wasn't maternal. So I came to think of her as a midwife, a doula, because what I felt her do with her body under my palms and fingers so keenly aware of the tender fibers of her cashmere hoodies was to lift me from one part of my life and gently, so gently, hold me as I moved myself to another.

"You carried me," I said to her once, in the moments we had after we knew her mind would go, and before it started to leave.

"Well, that's not exactly it," she said. "I feel more that I just held you while you changed."

And it was that that was so surprising and so magic. I had never been touched or held with a kind of pure and untrammeled love before, a love that wasn't clouded by anxieties, or by sexual desire, or by the awkwardness of being in a young body that doesn't know how to touch, or that— most important—didn't request anything of me. Over time, over the months that we spent together, our bodies learned to curl into each other's and over each other's. One night as we hugged good night, we kissed on the mouth, just gently and briefly and for less than a second, and it was a kiss of the kind I see now between mothers and their young children, and yet it came without that clarity of category. I was, at first, the active one—the person who picked up food, who fixed the Roku, who walked Sadie. But it was Allison who held me, who made herself a bulwark of delicacy and strength against which my body first floundered, and then came, finally, to rest.

two

~

From the time I could understand language, I knew that I would be sent away. My mother, a philosopher, had been raised by her mother, a neuroscientist, to know that she would one day be sent away. My mother's family sent everyone they could to a Quaker boarding school in Pennsylvania, and then away to college, either an Ivy League or close enough. As a young child I understood that I too would one day leave, that a rite of my childhood would be an early departure out the door, first for boarding school and then for college. Everything in my life was oriented toward future achievement; the steps were laid out even if the ultimate goal felt (moderately) open. I could be a professor of English or perhaps a professor of history. A professor of Shakespeare or a professor of classics. When we talked about my future, it was clear that there were tracks, specific tracks, laid out; partnership, friendship, intimacy weren't on these tracks. I cannot remember a single instance of being encouraged to make friends, though I can remember many instances of being asked to read advanced philosophy, or to write a paper "for fun!" on the nineteenth-century ethicist John Stuart Mill, or to sit quietly in my mother's philosophy department after school, making bookshelf labels of philosophers' names.

I was given bookshelves and asked questions about ideas instead of being given telephone privileges and asked questions about my friends. The students that I met in school—the Waldorf school in Eugene, Oregon, the private junior high school in Edmonton, Canada, and the others in between—were seen by my parents as impediments on the way toward progress, toward following the expected track. Friendships were obstructions to my progress, impositions to my plans (my family's plans?). I was born with the overt and constant pressure of being the product of two great minds, and so from the time that I could read, the time that I could speak, the time that I could write one word and then string it to the next one, I was told over and over and over again that someday I would do something amazing. All on my own.

~

My mother has been married three times. First to my father, a brilliant philosopher who made his way out of Grants Pass, Oregon, to get a PhD and eventually to become an endowed professor at an East Coast liberal arts college. Their marriage lasted five years, until I was one. Second to my stepfather Alex, who was finishing his PhD in philosophy at the University of Konstanz when my mother moved to Germany on a short-term research fellowship, two-year-old me in tow. I don't remember a time that I didn't know him, didn't see him as my father figure. My first memory is of watching my mother fall off a horse. She spent twelve weeks in a German hospital, resting so that her spine would knit itself back together, and Alex, who had thought he didn't want children, parented me alone for those twelve weeks. He took me to visit her, and, as he told me later, I turned away from the hospital's doors, didn't want to go in, tried to leave as soon as we got there. I remember the brightness of the hospital room and the powerlessness I felt over the fact of my mother's lying there. I remember the needlepoint that she did to pass the time. I remember the helplessness. I remember it being difficult to speak English. I remember it being difficult to speak. I also remember Alex's kindness.

A year after my mother and Alex married in a small ceremony in a small church in a small Bavarian town, my brother was born. When I was six and he was still a newborn our newly constructed family left Germany and moved back to Oregon, where I went to a creative school where we drew with crayons to learn math, crocheted rabbits and cup holders, built construction projects. It was an ideal place for me in terms of education: individualized attention, creative play, a single teacher who stayed with us even as we moved up grades. The school had a huge field, and on it we all pretended to ride imaginary horses, we ran after each other, we played cops and robbers, we gathered in the brambles behind a clearing, we hid behind trees and threw sticks. Even though I was barely sentient, I already felt that I was on the periphery, that everyone else was connecting in a way I fundamentally couldn't.

Not long after, we moved from Oregon to Canada, where

my mother had been made chair of a philosophy department and Alex was hired as a professor. We sent our furniture ahead in a truck, then drove north in three days, my brother and me in the back seat of the car, dividing our space with one suitcase, other suitcases below our feet. What I remember of that trip is a hike up the Columbia Glacier and sitting cross-legged in the back of a hot car. Arriving in Canada in July and being shocked that there was no snow, that Edmonton, our new home, was just a city like all the other cities I'd ever been to, with houses. I'd expected forests, the tundra of my American geography books, something utterly different from the landscape of my birth. Instead we encountered suburban sprawl, a city that began twenty minutes away from the airport and edged itself into existence, a strip mall leading to a shopping center leading to an indoor mall leading to neighborhoods with Victorian houses and leafy streets. We rented a house and then bought a house, and I went to a public school and then a private school, and then my brother went to that private school, and then I could feel the tracks of my future begin to unfold.

When I was twelve, my mother divorced Alex and married my second stepfather, Vishaan. He moved into our house and brought with him objects and habits that were surprising and thrilling: four-foot-tall stereo speakers that played opera at a volume we'd never have been allowed to turn the dial to; Indian and Italian cookbooks and the dishes they suggested; a temper that flared, quickly. He knew we liked well-done meat and cooked it rare every time. He brought with him parlor games, like one he invented where we went around the dinner table and each said what we most disliked about each other, or another game where we offered each other suggestions for improvement. We learned to wrap our suggestions around compliments, to never risk his wrath.

Our house had wood-lined rooms that were detailed with spectacular brocade wallpaper, gorgeously finished wooden floors, a kitchen with wide windows overlooking a sunny backyard. There were enough bedrooms for there to be an office and a sunroom and a bedroom for Vishaan's daughters, for when they came to visit. Our house had once appeared in a made-for-TV movie called *Small Sacrifices,* a fact I clung to. When I was home alone I pretended that I was in a movie, that someone was filming me walking down the stairs, into the kitchen. I walked down the stairs again and again, not to get anywhere, but to practice for a future in which people would want to watch me walk down stairs. I felt like I didn't fully exist for my parents; the solace was that one day I could exist for thousands of others. The dining room had a baby grand piano and a large old wooden table and a mahogany sideboard in which there were two sets of silver and the new china that he and my mother had received from one of the many department guests at their hastily planned wedding. We always ate dinner at 7:30 on the dot, and there was the suggestion of warmth that came from the candles we lit every night, from the turning down of the overhead light, but it was a suggestion that never came to fruition. I don't remember much laughter, or warmth, or easy togetherness. My brother and I were summoned with a bell and then expected to perform either quiet politeness or perfect diction. Mostly we spent the time pushing radicchio around our plates, glancing toward each other, while my mother and Vishaan talked to each other over the long end. We heard about teaching loads, papers, conferences;

the world of academia—the world behind the public face of scholarship—was the waterfall of our everyday life.

∾

Once, he hit me. The next day, someone, seeing a bruise: "Did you walk into a door?"

Yes, yes, I must have.

∾

At school I was part of a group of girls, the nerds. We shared a single black notebook full of notes that we sent back and forth between us.

I have a crush on Tom and he talked to me yesterday and I think that I want to talk to him. I would like at least one page of advice. —— Stephanie

I wrote a page of advice, the kind of advice a ninth-grader who's been reading both the *Sweet Valley High* series and Nabokov and has never been given any kind of Talk would give. Like:

*I totally think you should talk to him!!! !!!!
I feel like we are all forever alone inside our own minds + I think it would be SO KEWL if u ended up Frenching him*

I wrote to my friends about everything to do with boys and nothing to do with how things were at home. But I noticed that when I went over to Stephanie's house, her mother sat down at the table with her and talked to her—about more than what she was learning. I wanted to go to Stephanie's house every day after school, but my mother was adamant about reciprocal invitations; I wasn't allowed to go to her house twice in a row without having her over to mine. Friendship had rules, I learned early. But inviting Stephanie was hazardous. I couldn't count on Vishaan being in a good mood or if he would shift like a cloud into darkness. I'd seen it happen; company was no guarantee of things working out for me. One night she'd come over for dinner, and I'd been excited that she was there, so I'd gotten hyper and talked a lot during dinner, and interrupted, and Vishaan had said I was being mouthy. He had excused me from the table in the middle of eating, sent me upstairs to my room, and continued the conversation with Stephanie. She left before I was allowed back out.

Vishaan's cruelty was shocking for and because of its casualness. Years later, after he and my mother divorced, I saw him once, for dinner, during a layover in Toronto. "Sherry and I fight a lot!" he said, smile wide, face beaming. He loved the fighting, loved talking about how he fought with his new girlfriend. For him, conflict seemed to be energizing, enlivening. For me, for years after I lived with him, I believed that romantic conflict was the only way to feel alive, to feel pleasure, to feel my face crack into a wide smile, to beam.

I couldn't tell anyone how scared I was to be at home. I didn't know how. And so began my separation from other people. My belief that all of my insides had to be kept secret.

∾

As a teenager, I was sent away, not to the Quaker school everyone else in my family had gone to and many more would end up going to, but across an ocean. Vishaan resented my family's connection to Quakerism, so instead I ended up at The Leys, a Methodist boarding school in Cambridge, England. I was placed in Fen House, a dorm where all the girls had been together for four years and newcomers were not embraced. But I was socially adopted by the house rebel, and together we snuck out of school to smoke cigarettes on the nearby meadow; we sat on the steps of the pool house and watched the world go by; we smuggled beers into our dorm rooms and laughed into the darkness.

Boarding school was where I learned how to fit in by being quiet. Eventually the cool girls got used to my being there, and while I wasn't fully embraced, I was accepted. I almost never spoke, terrified that I would say the wrong thing (I'd had a few missteps early on: referring to trousers as "pants" and therefore asking to borrow a fellow student's underwear, asking for "corn" in the cafeteria and therefore accidentally requesting . . . animal feed). But I loved my classes, particularly my literature classes with Mr. Hopkins, who was short and passionate and who railed, one memorable day, against the "cool attitude" that he thought we were all trying to take toward books. Too shy to fight but so excited not to be alone in my deep affinity for reading, I hung on every word of his diatribe, and when everyone else left after class to laconically make fun of him, I stayed behind to tell him, eyes fixed on his desk, how much I agreed with him. I joined the Literary Society, which most of the members joined because it was an excuse to drink school-provided wine on a school night (liquor flowed at our school the way cigarettes and pot flow everywhere else), but which I joined because I thought I could finally find my tribe of book-obsessed readers.

I went for the books but I became hooked by the alcohol. Once I started drinking, I was able to access some different Eva, some other Eva. One Archers peach schnapps and lemonade in, and suddenly I was funny and the world made sense to me, and when Hugo Tischler, one of the coolest and most elusive kids in school, sat down next to me and said, "I'd like to get to know you," I knew that I had arrived.

∾

While I was in boarding school in England, my father and I reconnected, first over email and then in long, circuitous phone conversations — me sitting by the pay phone in Fen, him sitting on his black leather sofa at home in America. We didn't know how to talk to each other as humans, so we spoke to each other as scholars. I was reading for A-levels, a series of intense exams that English students intending to go on to college take, and I was preparing for tests in theology, German, and English.

My father and I spent hours talking about *The Tempest;* I read him the papers I wrote about Andrew Marvell's "The Garden." I told him about Mr. Hopkins, my passionate English teacher, and also about Mr. Birkin, who ran the Literature Society. We talked about transitional sentences, and the five-body-paragraph rule (and how much we disliked it). We talked about the problems of translation, the limits of ekphrasis. We talked about everything we could possibly find to talk about besides the only question that ever mattered: why he'd left, and why he'd stayed gone.

My father asked me to visit him and his new girlfriend, Leila, during my next summer break, and I did, and it was good, but dissipated, and over too quickly, and nothing was really said. It was a week of TV watching, errand running, ice cream buying. A week of not saying the things I wanted to say. A week of pretending that everything about this situation was not only normal but what I wanted.

And then I went back to England, where I took my A-levels and applied to a few colleges and then found myself at Princeton, where my first year I made some friends but not that many, where I tried to find my people, where once again I felt alone. After my first year my father offered to find me an internship at his college, asking if I could perhaps come and live with him for the summer. I couldn't wait.

I came with the hope of making a connection with my father that summer; instead, I fell in love with Leila. She was living with him, in between things, was having a summer off during grad school, where she was studying philosophy. And so she was chilling at his house, working on applications or maybe a paper or . . . I have no idea, because she seemed so much older than me. But she took to me and I to her. She was funny, and dry, and had been born in the UK to two Thai parents and then grown up in Texas, so she was a British citizen with an Austin background. She was part of a group of artistic friends, silk-screeners and museum curators and writers, who sometimes came to dinner at my father's house, who prompted me to give long disquisitions on architectural history, who thought it was cute when I got a little hammered on Heineken and couldn't clearly articulate the difference between the modernist Philip Johnson and the modernist Mies van der Rohe, both of whom were known for their (slightly different) glass boxes. Leila had a self-confidence that I envied, a sense of rightness with the world. She knew she was smart, she knew she was good at reading, she knew her ideas were powerful, she knew she was funny. She watched the right movies and listened to the right music. She loved Radiohead; she took me to my first concert. She had ties to New York City, to London, to San Francisco. She was good enough at philosophy that she was pursuing a PhD. She was everything I'd ever wanted to be.

I had started smoking in England and kept smoking at Princeton, and she realized that I was smoking even as my father didn't, and she smoked too, and so she and I would sneak outside to the end of the condo driveway and smoke cigarettes together. She introduced me to Billy Blanks's Tae Bo videos, which we followed together in the airy living room, me feeling emboldened by her unselfconscious enthusiasm for his punch sequences. She opened a beer for me when I came home from a long day at the construction site where my internship was; the rules were that I could drink at home, as much as I wanted, so long as I never drank anywhere else. To supplement my unpaid internship, I'd gotten a paying job working at Subway, and she made fun of my visor and green T-shirt and at the same time praised me for going to work.

Leila became the glue between my father and me. I still didn't know why he'd left when I was a baby, didn't understand why he had almost never visited me when I was growing up. My contact with him was, as far as I can remember, limited to Christmas presents that never quite suited me but that I decided I loved—tiny backpacks a year after Prada brought them in and out of style, a leather coat that I wore every single day even though the waist sat on my rib cage, a guitar. Because of the emotional reticence with which I'd been raised, I'd never felt comfortable telling him how much his absence had hurt, had never asked him why he'd been gone, but Leila knew enough to know that this girl who was suddenly living in her boyfriend's house and really interested in sneaking outside to smoke, and drinking as much as possible, was probably having a very awkward time of things.

"So . . . things seem pretty weird this summer," she said to me one day while we were outside smoking. "I feel like maybe you need to work some things out with your dad?"

No one had ever told me I needed to work something out with him. No one had ever told me I needed to work something out with anyone. My mother had been elusive on the topic of my father and their separation; Alex, who had been my parent—even post-divorce—for as long as I could remember, hadn't brought him up that much, not wanting to confuse me; and Vishaan had basically refused to acknowledge his existence.

In the end it would take years to work things out with my father. It would take therapy, and more therapy, and his marrying someone else, whom I also fell in love with, and time, and false starts, and fits, and arguments, and carefully worded conversations, and backslides, and leaps, and trying, always trying. The important thing wasn't that Leila got me to figure things out with him. The important thing was that Leila was the first person to ever see the depth of my pain and loneliness and awkwardness, to see that I was struggling with something, and then to love me in spite of and maybe even *for* it, and to show me where I could grow. From the first months that I spent with her, Leila nudged me into a larger life. Carried me while I tried to get myself from one place to another. Just like Allison would.

~

During my junior year, they called me.

"We have some sad news," they said, both of them on the line.

"We've decided to separate," they said.

"We both love you very much, and this has nothing to do with you," they said.

I'd been through two divorces by then but had never been brought into the conversation like this. It felt like a punch. I let myself cry for a beat or two, and then I laughed.

"I'm just really sad," I said.

And then, an attempt at control: "Sorry I cried — that was kinda dramatic."

"It's really sad," they said. "It's okay to cry."

I hung up.

A few weeks later, I stopped attending class. I went to the dean and asked for an extension for my final assignments.

"My stepmother and dad are divorcing," I said. It was a half-truth. She wasn't my stepmother. Yes, they were separating. Yes, it was affecting me. But I also knew I was using this as an excuse to give myself more time to do better in school (my grades were slipping; drugs were coming in). But the way I was playing it made it seem like she had raised me. Like she was family.

Years later, I would realize how true that was.

~

As our lives went on, Leila and I kept in middling touch. I graduated from college with a degree in architecture that was moderately useless considering I can't draw and have no sense of spatial creativity. But it proved to be useful in kick-starting a career as an architectural writer, and so I moved to New York City to work in publishing and write about architecture, and she was relatively close by, in Philadelphia for law school, where she'd gone after dropping out of her PhD program. She kept up our relationship by emailing me every few weeks, calling me every few months. And so, newly independent, without a real job or any real commitments, every so often I took the train to visit her, and we went to clubs or restaurants or bars, and every time, I got too drunk.

My getting too drunk was starting to become a theme. I was getting too drunk in front of my coworkers, my roommate, my boss. I had a job as an editorial assistant at a publishing house, where I photocopied manuscripts and called for messengers and read the slush pile. I was also working as a researcher for an author who was under contract to write a book, and so I was seeing both sides of the industry. The beginning of the week I spent in the publishing offices, photocopying and loitering. On Thursdays and Fridays I went to the writer's apartment in Carroll Gardens, sifted through newspaper clippings, and most of all I watched the writing process, how he went from a chapter outline to a few pages to, a year later, printed-out chapters lined up against the wall of a Brooklyn studio he'd rented first to have a writing space and then, after he told his wife that he was in love with me, a place to sleep. Sometimes with me.

~

To sleep there was to betray not only the writer's wife, but also what I had built—and precipitously left—with my college boyfriend, Tim, whom I'd met my junior year and fallen into an easy partying-and-pot-fueled relationship with. Tim was a musician, a singer and guitarist, and he was kind and gentle and everyone liked him, and because he was so nice, they were nice to me. I loved him sometimes desperately and sometimes casually. It was my easiest relationship, and also my most detached. We were friends, and lovers, and we lived together in New York, first with others and then just together, and he drifted into getting stoned every day and I drifted into staying out late every night, and soon we were passing ships. We were in the same social circle, and so when we broke up, messily and mostly because of the writer, I distanced myself from our shared college friends and got closer to the writer and his friends, who were all in their midthirties, married men, some of whom had different codes, and any moral compass I might have tried to learn from Tim disappeared.

Why had I learned a moral compass from Tim? I had come to college full of ideas about life that I'd picked up mostly from my parents' well-stocked bookshelves and whatever I could observe of their behavior. We didn't participate in church or any kind of religious organization, beyond occasional attendance at Quaker meetings when we were visiting my grandparents on the East Coast. Years later, watching friends of mine parent their children, teaching them about sharing, or gentleness, or waiting, I wondered why that level of teaching felt so foreign to me; like I'd missed out on it. I couldn't remember growing up with any kind of education about social responsibility, any turn toward service, or helping others, beyond a vague sense that we should protest wars and that violence was never the answer. In fifth grade, we were required by my elementary school to volunteer; the options were a retirement home or an animal shelter. I chose the retirement home, where I visited an eighty-six-year-old woman named Julianne once a week, told her about my classes and books I was reading (some habits came early). She saved candy for me; I read the newspaper to her. I saw her every Tuesday for two months, and then she died. Our teacher announced it in class. I sobbed quietly in my seat from shock and grief; it was the first and last time for over a decade that I cried in public. Years later, my mother would see my friendship with Allison as another example of this kind of predilection toward hanging out with sick old women. But that wasn't it, not with Julianne, and not with Allison. It was that I was born with love to give and had never been told where to put it.

As a child, I was given some rules, yes: say please and thank you, wash your hands before dinner, make eye contact when you pass the salt (with, always, the pepper). But I wasn't given a deeper underlying moral theory to explain the rules about reciprocity and politeness that I was offered. As I entered college and then graduated and then saw how we all fumbled around in New York in our early twenties, trying to teach each other and tell each other the rules we'd either grown up with or read about or experimented with in our post-dark peregrinations, I wondered if it was possible that I didn't come to my relationship with Tim without a clear moral compass of my own not because of something deeply and intractably wrong with me, or even with the way I'd been raised, but because of the particular time in which we all grew up: between the Baby Boom and the progressive crisis of the early twenty-first century; between the promise of the American Dream and its loss.

Tim at least pretended to know the rules. He broke up with me the summer after our first year together, our junior year of college.

"It doesn't make sense to stay together for the summer," he said. "Everyone breaks up between school years."

I didn't want to break up, not at all, but I agreed, because I figured I was supposed to agree, and this was probably a rule I just didn't know about, and then when I believed in the break and kissed someone else and told Tim, he fell silent, then enraged.

"I can't believe you cheated on me," he said.

But hadn't he broken up with me? I believed that the problem wasn't one of two young adults having no fucking clue what to do. I believed the problem was that I just wasn't getting it right. And so as my neural architecture solidified, as my frontal cortex began to lock itself into place, I looked to fictional worlds to help me understand the moral rules of engagement in the real world. The only problem was that fictional thought experiments didn't translate to real-world humans. I read about fidelity, affairs, the interior moral landscape and the exterior one. I read about what it meant to have a good relationship, and what a bad one looked like. But no matter how many books I read, I still couldn't connect theory with reality.

One night, in a bar, after Tim and I had repaired things, gotten back together, graduated, and moved to New York to live together in a tiny East Village walk-up, I asked a friend for his thoughts about fidelity. Why was it so different to touch someone's arm instead of his mouth? I understood, for instance, that cheating was bad because it might hurt the person being cheated on; I wasn't *truly* a sociopath. But if the person never found out, was it still bad? Was it so bad to touch someone else's mouth with your mouth instead of his hand with your hand? And if yes, as most of the people I knew seemed to agree, then why? It's not that I wanted to be polyamorous. I didn't. I wanted monogamy. But I couldn't stop myself from burrowing into pockets of my mind that were outside of the rules we were teaching each other. Moments of feeling like anything that only I — and a stranger — experienced weren't real, didn't count. Did others feel this? I never asked. I wish I had.

When things fell apart with Tim, I turned to my mentor: the writer. He had different rules, looser rules, more flagrant rules, and I liked them. He and I were together for two years, and in those two years I isolated myself even further from my college friends, who had gone from central to my life while I was with Tim to the periphery. I tried to keep up with a few of them, individually, but it was hard to find common ground, particularly once I went from being a monthly cocaine user to a biweekly cocaine user to a weekly cocaine user to an almost daily cocaine user. The further I slid into alcoholism and addiction, the harder it was for me to remember who I'd been to these friends in college, or to imagine who I'd been to them. The truth is that they were kinder to me, more morally expansive, than I recognized at the time. The truth that I found out later is that, when I disappeared, they missed me. But I was busy falling into despair, as I transformed from someone who realized that I drank too often but could probably slow down if I really wanted to, to someone who kept getting into increasingly precarious situations like interviewing world-renowned architects through a haze of not-sleeping + alcohol + cocaine + hangover + a little proverbial hair of the (cocaine + alcohol) dog.

The irony, of course, is that I was desperate to connect, and that I believed that getting drunk or high with the people around me would forge a friendship, a deepening. The writer called cocaine my truth serum for how quickly, once I'd done a line or five, I started talking as honestly as I could, disarmed myself from the mantle of quietness or alert observation or egocentric self-bolstering that I'd otherwise tend toward. During the day, before I accidentally got too drunk, I played myself up as wildly successful: writing for the *New York Times,* incredibly young to have as many bylines as I did. I'd been a terrible designer in school; my ego loved that my teachers, who hadn't given me much attention during our studios, were now in a position where I could write about them. I was drunk not only on alcohol but on the promise of the adjacent power that comes from being able to believe, if you stretch the truth, that you can make someone famous. But as soon as I got drunk and high, a different version of my life came out. More truths were revealed. Like that I was terrified of what it meant to be published, that I worried every second that I'd made some kind of unforgivable—and eternally traceable—error. I oscillated between the desire to have my name in print and the terror that once my name was in print, I would be seen. I oscillated between my desperation to be noticed and my desire to live in the shadows. I believed at once that no one was reading me and that everyone I knew was reading me. "I recognize your byline" became something I heard, but it was never followed with anything. Did it mean my interlocutor had liked my article on couples who chose to live with a roommate? Did it mean he had hated my piece on an expensive Connecticut house? As a child, I'd had dreams of using language to begin to shape the world, but I was starting to feel that my contributions —which were, to be fair, more about expensive apartments for wealthy people than the emphasis on social housing I'd focused on in college—weren't actually mattering. I flipped between two intractable and inconsistent extremes: I was wildly important; I barely existed.

Alcohol was supposed to give me that sense of intimacy that would let me know I existed. But of course, once I was drunk, I couldn't actually connect. My days and weeks and then months and then years became a merry-go-round of desperation and failure, blanketed by my fundamental belief that if I were just myself, unaltered, in all my insecurity and confusions and hopes and worries and fears, no one would love me.

Eventually I realized that I couldn't go on like this. That it was only getting worse. That I wasn't outgrowing my inability to get so shitfaced on Tuesdays that I missed copyeditors' calls on Wednesdays. That if I kept drinking the way I was drinking, I would die. I missed the clarity and simplicity of the life I'd had with Tim. Even if we'd become passing ships, I'd understood the framework of our relationship. I hadn't really understood why the rules were the way they were, but I'd been able to trust that they existed. Things with the writer were full of surprises, emotional whiplash, bar fights, and dramatic infidelities. Our performance of a wild couple had become reality, and it wasn't as much fun to wake up to as it had been to fantasize about. I missed my college friends. I didn't know how to get back to them. A late morning after a long night, numb with shock at a relationship breach, fingering the tiny bag of cocaine in my pocket, trying not to become one of those people who *did drugs during the day,* a rule I had set for myself to try to deny to myself the encroaching fact that I was an addict, that I couldn't leave the house without drugs, and feeling I had nowhere else to turn, I called Leila. She was the only person I could think of who would still help me.

She had moved to New York and was working as a lawyer downtown. The night I called her we met for dinner at Brooklyn Fish Camp, a restaurant in Park Slope. I know now how many things she had to rearrange to be free on that short notice. I described to her what my life had become. The most recent fight with the writer. How lost I felt. How tied to him — his money, his apartment that we shared, his family — I felt. The waiter came by, asked if we wanted some wine.

"I have like half a gram of blow and a bottle of wine I'm trying to get out of my system," I said to her.

"I think she's good with water," Leila said to the waiter.

She turned back to me.

"So what do you want to do?"

As desperately as I wanted to change, I also couldn't see my way into the next steps. I knew I should stop drinking, but I couldn't figure out how. I knew I wanted to stop the way that being able to feel a bag of cocaine in my pocket was the only thing that gave me a sense of safety. She had some ideas.

"Maybe you should stop doing drugs?" she said.

"I know," I said. "I *know.*"

And then: "But how?"

And then she extended herself—our friendship—in the biggest way imaginable. A pause while our lobster rolls arrived.

"I think you should come home with me," she said.

And so that's what I did, spending months sleeping on her air mattress, pushing her generosity as far as it could go, while I attempted to dry myself out. While I deleted first one dealer's number and then the next and then, finally, a few months later, my favorite dealer's of all. While I tried to change.

"What's your plan?" she finally asked. I heard the subtext. The subtext had been that I wasn't supposed to be living there for three months; I was supposed to have crashed there for a few weeks while things evened out, while I found my own place. But things hadn't evened out. I didn't have any money, and it was 2007, and the economy wasn't crashing yet but I had apparently crashed my own economy in the run-up to getting sober (the night, they say, is darkest just before the dawn), and so I had no work, was basically unemployable. Interviews that I had missed without explanation or rescheduling because of hangovers had started to work their way back to commissioning editors; I wasn't young enough anymore for it to be cute (it had never been cute). After meeting the writer I had left my part-time publishing job in favor of full-time freelancing, had experienced a relatively meteoric ascent, and then I had crashed and burned and now, here, was nothing.

When I'd had connections (all through the writer) to many respected publications, I'd been part of a larger publishing orbit. I had repeated my high school and college practice of being adjacent to the cool kids, and when I'd been doing blow with *Gawker* writers in Lower East Side apartments, I'd figured people had liked me. But now that I was desperately trying to do anything besides blow, what did I have to talk to anyone about? Now that I wasn't playing a part, the role of the ingénue with the remarkable success and the completely unpredictable home life, what part could I play? Myself? What was myself? At a party, a few months after I got sober, as I was sipping on club soda, someone asked me what I liked to do for fun. I couldn't think of a single example. Once my ambition had kicked into full gear and found grist in the mill of early-twenty-first-century New York City publishing, I had lost any internal sense of self I might have slowly amassed over my college years. Desperate for the love that I believed success would give me, I'd made what seemed now like nonsensical choices. I'd traded in friendships for a byline; had skipped birthday parties to go to openings where I'd thought I might meet the next editor who would give me the next assignment that would finally prove that I was valuable. Was everyone else like this? This combination of ambition and hunger felt like the tip of some kind of secret that we were all in on; except I just wasn't sure what the secret really was. Was it that we were all actually competing? That we were all faking it? I didn't want to admit to myself that I treated social interactions as steps on the ladder, but I did, and in a way it's because New York, at that time, taught me to do that. Because Princeton, with its system of socially hierarchical eating clubs, had taught me how to navigate power. Being a writer in New York took the tiny spark of ambition I'd always had and threaded wires around it and attached it to some C4 explosive, and there I was. Part of the momentum was mine. Part of the momentum was the internet's. We didn't yet have the inward focus that we have now. There were no guided meditation groups at MoMA, fewer yoga studios, no turmeric lattes. The crisis of late-stage capitalism that we entered into after the 2008 recession, the one that sent us all to Adorno's magic horoscopes, yoga teacher trainings, and Peruvian plant medicine retreats hadn't happened yet, not to us.

But something was happening to me. I had no money. No stability. No connections to call on. No friends beyond Leila to ask for help. (Or I did, but my shame was too strong.) Over the years, I had at first gradually and then suddenly cut off everyone with whom I'd had an uncomfortable interaction, and by the point in my drinking that I knew I had to get sober, that was almost everyone I'd had *any* kind of interaction with. The intimacy of having to show how publicly and spectacularly I believed I had failed not only others but myself was terrifying. I couldn't do it.

Instead of reaching out for help, I disappeared myself—into dating a new guy, Charles. Into Leila's air mattress. Into trying to decide what to do with the five dollars I had left to get me through the week. And finally, into my body. I lost fifteen pounds the first month I stayed with her, and checked the scale every morning, reveling in the numbers as they went down: 130, 125, 121, 117, 115. I loved being below 120, loved the feeling of pulling on jeans without even unbuttoning them, sliding them over my sharp hipbones, feeling the hollow of my belly when I lay down. My hands and fingers felt delicate for the first time. I became obsessed with my own body, with looking at it in Leila's bathroom mirror. My body became a type of sanctuary, its own place of reprieve. I wasn't fully occupying it, not like I would later, but I was next to it, close enough to see it even if I couldn't feel what it was like to be inside. Even though I was physically starving I never felt hungry; occasionally I felt nauseated, or tired, but it was then that my physical appetite disappeared.

~

Later, I knew that this was the first symptom.

~

But then, I knew only the pride I felt when my shorts slipped off my body, and the fear I felt that Leila—Leila, who had time and time again given me a safe place to land, who had asked what my plan was as a way of starting a conversation, not of ending one—would kick me out.

Pride and fear. The two bugbears that have kept themselves on my shoulders even until now.

~

I went to Charles. "I need to move out of Leila's within two weeks," I told him. (My deadline, not Leila's.) He didn't offer to have me move in.

"It should be easy for you to find a place," he said.

I thought about it. I had no rental history; I'd been living with the writer for two years, living off him. I had no income. I had no money in my bank account, nothing for a security deposit, or rent. I felt completely helpless. And instead of going back to Leila, to her warm apartment and her friendship and her acceptance of me, I doubled down on this. On not needing to ask a friend for help. On manipulating my way out of a situation. So I performed vulnerability, thought about what I had to trade: the leverage of a romantic relationship, the subtle promise of sex. I cried. He crossed the room and held me and said, "Okay, you can move in for a few weeks while you figure something out."

I lived with Charles for my first sober year, in a tiny backyard Brooklyn studio that he had renovated, a two-story structure with a catwalk that went around the second floor, its cantilever hovering precipitously over the ground floor, where his bed, which he had also built himself, could be rearranged to turn into an art surface. I felt distance with him but also closeness, because I had met him in a very romantic way — on an art retreat in upstate New York, next to a sculpture of his that was called, perhaps not incidentally, *End End End* — and I was living out some sort of personal fantasy: me the writer, him the artist, making our greatest works.

I read the few assignments I was still writing out loud to him as he glued pieces of paper to other pieces of paper. His constructions were always iterative, building on each other, profoundly formalist. His biggest piece was a sculpture called *Finish Line,* made of thousands of Styrofoam blocks that he laboriously glued together. He spent hours at the studio every day, methodically gluing one piece to the next to the next. I had never worked, or even thought, that way. I was impulsive, slap-dash, too close to the deadline. I loved precipitous decisions and precarious decisions—interviewing an architect in a crowded bar with a tape recorder about to run out of battery (some of this happened in the early 2000's; we used tape recorders). I was chronically late, harried, frazzled, stressed. He was so calm and measured that it came through in his symmetrical, theoretically informed work. The real art, he always said to me, was in the things he had thought about while gluing these blocks together: the rise of minimalism, the art of Robert Morris, the relationship between film and sculpture.

My relationship with Charles felt like a complete counterweight to the one that had come before. Charles was warm. He loved me. He was stable.

"I'm dedicated to you," he said one night after I'd expressed a fleeting insecurity. "I want to marry you."

And yet it wasn't enough. It could never be enough. Because that glue, that connection, that sense of trust that I saw other people have with each other—I didn't know how to have that. I felt far away, locked into myself, to my own thoughts and fears and worries. I felt braided into a set of beliefs about myself: that I was unknowable; that I was unlovable; that I was fundamentally wired to be alone.

Sometimes, lying in bed together at night, me forcing myself to come back to where I was, to his room, to his bed, my soul trying to fly out of my body, to safety somewhere else/ somewhere farther away, he noticed.

"Where are you?" he said. "You feel so distant." It was something I'd heard before, from other people. Would hear again. "Like you're behind ice."

A year and a half after we met at his sculpture, we broke up. Spectacularly. I went on a press trip and I met someone and he seemed exciting and most of all he took me out of myself when he took me into his room, and that moment of connection became a moment of disconnection. For all of my reading about it, infidelity in practice was a way for me to carve out my own space in the world, to remind myself that I existed. It opened up the world for me to a sense of hidden chambers and secrets, pockets of decision and experience and choice that I stitched together to create some sense of solid ground. I believed that if I could string enough of these together, I could begin to make sense of my life. And yet every one led to some terrible destruction, some excruciating pain that I couldn't understand.

three

~

Three years after I left Charles, four years of staying sober and going to rooms and slowly, slowly, slowly beginning to rearrange the way I was in the world, I met Cameron, in the same room in which I met Allison. I saw her across the room, a spring day during my first year in graduate school at Berkeley, the semester after the semester I first met Allison and watched movies with her, and the second I saw Cameron—this was love at first sight, this time for real —I wanted to be close to her, next to her, wanted to hear what she said, and most of all I wanted to touch her face, her body. I wanted to run my hands along her arms and over her torso, wanted to clamp my palm on to the back of her neck and pull her face to mine. I wanted to be in her orbit, her aura. She had short dark hair and deep brown eyes. I was entranced. The day we met, she was wearing a button-down blue shirt, its paleness contrasting with the depth of her eyes, and everything about her face was symmetrical and, to me, perfect. Her jaw line was strong, her nose angu-

lar. Her mouth was the most perfectly formed mouth I had
ever seen.

She walked over to me and asked me if I liked science fiction movies, to which I said of course I did, and she asked
if I wanted to watch a movie, and so on our first date we
went to the open-air mall close to campus to buy a cord that
would attach my computer to my television, building a cord
that would begin to attach ourselves to each other, borrow-
ing her friend's bright blue Volvo, blue to match her eyes and
her shirt, and then to the grocery store, where we flirted and
then we watched a movie and our arms touched and then our
hands were grazing each other's forearms, and then I kissed
her and then everything took over and I took her into the
bedroom and everything in my body felt like it was on fire.

This was the feeling I had looked for when I had been
with men, and one I'd gotten only if the relationship was
new or the circumstances were extreme: if they were cheating, or if I was cheating, or if this wasn't supposed to be happening, or if they were slapping me in the face, or calling me
a whore, or tying me up, or coming in my hair. Only then
could I feel alive, only then could I feel a fire. And yet with
Cameron I felt the fire from everything.

Sex was disembodied for me, almost entirely, until I met
Cameron. And then sex with her was so embodied that the
fire, our fire, her fire, my fire, felt like it was inexhaustible,
unextinguishable. One night, ten days or a week or five days
after we'd met, and so ten times or seven times or five times
that we'd had sex, she fell onto me and "I love you" fell out of
her mouth as her face fell onto mine. I loved her too because
my body loved her, because my body responded to her like it
had never responded to anyone's, and because my body felt

like it belonged to her, and maybe because her body was so similar to mine—light, lithe, same height, same build, same bone structure, soon same haircut—that it felt like my body belonged to myself. After a lifetime spent feeling that my body was an abstraction, the vessel that carried my ideas, I finally felt what it was to be this alive.

And then, just as quickly, the light went out. For us, and for my body. We spend the rest of the relationship trying to break up.

As soon as we moved in together, the sex stopped, replaced with near-constant conversation, deflection, muted desire turned into aggression. She criticized me for being too loud, too messy, too sloppy, for eating too much candy and chocolate. I criticized her for being too reserved, too quiet, too straightforward. She criticized my sobriety. I criticized her choice, after ten years sober, to drink. She criticized my cooking, I criticized her belief that she needed to be gluten-free. We saw a therapist together, who suggested that our chakras were incorrectly aligned, and then we saw another therapist together, who suggested that we were in a dance of approach and withdrawal, and then we stopped seeing therapists together. My body became a topic. I'd gained weight my first year of grad school, and so I was too fat. I lost twenty pounds. I was too thin. I didn't work out enough. I should do more yoga. I should do less yoga. I had committed to her so quickly and so strongly and so publicly that I felt trapped, and so of course I started flirting with a member of my writing seminar, and of course I retreated into a world of silence and questioning the rules and almost, almost kissing him one night, and then, just as soon as I'd started betraying my body once again, my body betrayed me.

∼

After I got sick, everyone asked a version of the same questions:

"How did it start? How did you know?"

First, two years into living with Cameron, a blackness rising into my eyes and a fall, in the hallway. Except that wasn't first, because first, a sense of something not being right, and then a fall. Except that isn't right either: it was first nausea, occasional abrupt, violent vomiting. But then, this first: a year earlier I'd been on a bicycle ride with hundreds of cyclists, riding from San Francisco to Los Angeles to raise money for AIDS research, and something had happened midride. I'd overheated or gotten too cold, I'd gotten dehydrated or overhydrated, I became disoriented and stopped at the tent and said *I need help, I can't make it,* but then I slept and decided to feel better and then the next day I got back on the bike. I have a picture of me that morning, wet and smiling and covered in rain and soon to be covered in Mylar because the ride was diverted that day because of rain and we were given Mylar blankets, but it wasn't enough for me; I had to leave the ride completely, abandon my bicycle to a truck that would take it down to Los Angeles and then back to San Francisco, and I checked into a Holiday Inn in Paso Robles, hundreds of miles from anywhere I knew, and slept for two days, too tired to walk, to move. I lived on milkshakes and grilled cheese from the diner across the parking lot, and why didn't I say something to someone? Why didn't I go to the emergency room? Why did I think I was going to be okay?

But then this first, before: In New York City, years earlier, when after losing my appetite and moving in with Charles and then breaking up with Charles and moving into a short-term Brooklyn apartment, I woke up dizzy and felt a catch in the back of my throat and never righted myself. Or maybe this first, in Leila's apartment, when my jeans started to slide down the sharp jut of my hipbones, or maybe it started before then, with skin and hands and itchiness, and if this were a story about a diagnostic mystery, here's where I would tell you all the names of the tests I had, the numbers I learned, and how useless they were.

But this, here, is a story about love—and so I was standing and then the world went black and then I fell in the hallway and Cameron slapped me awake and I was nauseated and so I called my school clinic doctor and asked for a Zofran prescription, because I remembered a morning of nausea on the bike ride and a Zofran under my tongue and how it had corrected the nausea, and my doctor agreed, called it in, and I couldn't figure out how to fill it, couldn't get off the floor of the pharmacy once I got there, couldn't stand up, couldn't read, and the nausea, again the nausea, and I was supposed to teach that afternoon. I almost went to class, but I didn't—some part of me knew that I needed to cancel, and so emergency room and so eventually hospitalization and eventually brain scan and eventually finding a hemorrhage and a mass and eventually consult for brain surgery.

I'd never had surgery, not for anything. And to start with the brain? All I could think to myself was *Go big or go home.*

The last time I saw Cameron was in front of UCSF, after my consult with Dr. Anand, the neurosurgeon (*my* neurosurgeon, I kept reminding myself; I was someone who now had a neurosurgeon). I had watched him point at a picture of a lesion on the posterior of my pituitary lobe—I was learning that the pituitary had two parts—and tell me there was a dark spot there and it should be bright, which meant some kind of mass was in the way, and there was also a thickening on the pituitary stalk, "thickening" often being an early indicator of tumor growth.

"And when we add that to the elevated AFP, well, it's pretty slam dunk," he said. He was looking at the screen instead of at me. We were both looking at the screen. The picture seemed an abstraction; it couldn't possibly be inside my head. It was unnerving that I couldn't see the injury without computers and screens. This wasn't like a sprained wrist or a broken elbow. The only reflection that something was even wrong required a complex combination of magnets, computer code, and the importance of a millimeter.

"Elevated AFP": this meant I had an elevated tumor marker, a marker that appeared in the blood only when a tumor that appeared either in the ovaries or in the brain (both are along the central nervous system line, they're so connected) was present. It was either that posterior pituitary dark spot or a tiny tumor along the stalk that was producing the AFP, he thought, but we couldn't biopsy the stalk—it was too dangerous, mortality too likely—so we had to hope it was that dark spot; this is what would be biopsied during the surgery. Hope for brain cancer to be in one place and not another. The scale of my life was shifting, fast. And then, I asked, what were the chances of complications, of disorder, of morbidity, of death?

"One percent chance you'll get a sinus infection afterward," he said. And other complications?

"One percent, one percent, less than one percent," he said, rattling them off. Diabetes insipidus, permanent brain damage, death.

What other complications could I have asked about? What complications could I possibly have known were coming? That my brain would take months to rewire itself? That it would take me years to recover? That I would come to consider the end of everything I thought I knew, every day?

Or that I would also, finally, through the way in which I was loved for the next four years, the next lifetime, even, find and build the self I had been so desperately searching for? That I would lose the life I'd always thought I wanted and get another one instead? That it would be this, this sickness, that would break me open? That it would take something so dramatic, so completely against my will, to shake me out of the insecurity and crushing self-judgment I'd lived with for decades? That I would come to feel that my experience with this pocket of my brain, this collection of neurons, had become a teacher who I would never have chosen but would never give back? That I would finally, finally feel what it was to be loved?

I didn't know an iota of what was to come. So instead, okay, okay, okay, yes, smiling, yes, thank you, thank you for your time, okay, okay, okay, what's the treatment, okay, chemotherapy and radiation, okay, okay, words I've heard from

Allison, words that apply to other people, words that don't apply to me.

So I said goodbye, and Cameron said that this was too dangerous, and I shouldn't do it, and what about her feelings; the consult was the relationship-breaking straw we both needed. I said goodbye again, and it was clear that it was final, and I made my way across town to the same room in which I'd met Allison, and I fell to the floor next to Allison's chair, desperate from grief at ending this relationship and overwhelmed at having been told my diagnosis was *a slam dunk for brain cancer,* and Allison touched my shoulder and my back and my other shoulder and whispered to me, "I'll take care of you, I got you, I got you."

◈

When I moved in with Allison, we thought it would be for a night or two. Then it became clear the breakup was sticking, that I needed her help. My body needed her. My mind, which appeared to have abandoned me since that hallway fall, needed her. I woke up in her back bedroom in the mornings devastatingly tired, stayed devastatingly tired all day. I was on an experimental course of nortriptyline, an old tricyclic antidepressant. One of the many doctors who swept through my hospital room had thought my symptoms—the fainting, the nausea, the confusion, the exhaustion—might be because of silent migraines, and so I took this pill, which lodged in my throat sometimes, which woke me up to a dissolving bitterness, and during the day I shivered and was hot, alternating between the two, sleeping every day from eleven a.m. until four p.m. and then again going to bed at eight p.m. and sleeping until ten a.m. What did I do? I remember watching *The Hills* on Netflix, on repeat, over and over and over again. It was hard to talk. It was hard to read. It was hard to follow anything. I was a PhD student at the top public university in the world, and the complexity of the subplots of *The Hills* was beyond me.

I wrote an email to some of my college friends and New York friends, telling them I had to get brain surgery. I made jokes, and deflected, and said I was sure I'd be fine even though I was sure I wouldn't be, and they wrote back either with stories of people they had known who'd had brain surgery, or telling me this was really intense and they were thinking of me. My freshman-year roommates sent me a Kindle, and a friend from New York sent me an Edible Arrangement, and it was tiny kindnesses like that that meant everything, though I couldn't really let them land, couldn't feel the power of what was behind the gifts. Letting everything in would have meant acknowledging the reality of what was happening. That I was getting this much attention because I needed it. Because I deserved it.

I took so many pictures of myself then, and later — selfies about to fall asleep, selfies about to get out of bed. I took pictures of me and Allison, and then just of Allison, and of her and Sadie and me and Sadie. I didn't post all of the pictures, but I took hundreds. I wanted to document what was happening, save it for later. To tell myself that there would be a later. I wanted to see myself reflected back to me. I wanted to know what I looked like now, in case I never looked like this again. In case the surgeon's knife slipped. In case I was thrown straight into eighteen months of chemotherapy. In case my brain needed to be radiated; in case the person I had begun stitching together in the years since I'd stopped drinking disappeared. One morning, I took a picture and then looked at my eyes, my nose, my eyebrows. It wasn't the same as seeing a reflection. In college, I'd looked at myself in the mirror some nights, trying to find myself in my eyes. "You're here, you're here, look at you," I'd whispered to myself, my nose dripping from cocaine, my throat raw from throwing up the ninth shot I'd taken. But here, looking at a picture of myself on my phone, I felt more present.

Presence was all I had. I couldn't do anything for anyone. I couldn't write, couldn't work. I couldn't teach. I couldn't help anyone. I couldn't follow the rules of reciprocity; I could only take. How to know that I existed? How to know that I mattered? Of course I had read articles that said that just *being* was enough. Of course someone had slipped me a Pema Chödrön book. Of course a therapist in New York had tried to convince me that what I saw as the perils of an ordinary life, something I was loath to even consider, were not in fact the pools of quicksand I believed they were. But here, now, all I could do was wait. Wait for pain, and what I was sure would be bad news. And so, click. A picture. I exist. Click. I exist. *Those are my eyes. That's my nose. That's my mouth, with its right-sided curve.*

Some of the pictures were just for me. Some were also for me, but in a different way. When I posted the pictures online, it was so that everyone else could remind me that I was still here. Could give me permission to feel the blank terror that permeated every breath. *See me,* I wanted to say. *See how afraid I am.*

I believed I couldn't say that. The pull of the narrative

that I was tough, and strong, and would get past this felt more powerful than the real story, the one that I felt building underneath, the one that felt more true. That I might not be as tough as I'd always thought. That I might not be as strong as my friends wanted to tell me I was. That I might not get past this.

See me. See me. I am so afraid.

Allison wasn't convinced by my occasional histrionics.

"Do you think I'm going to die?" I asked her.

"*I'm* going to die," she said. "I have metastasized breast cancer that's gone to my liver and my bones."

"Right, but what about me?" I was so panicked, even if technically I didn't have more than one percent of a reason to be, that I couldn't comprehend what she was telling me.

"I don't think so, babe," she said. Her clarity stung. I was kinda digging this moment at the edge, hard as it was. That freedom I'd been looking for? I didn't think it would work so well if I was just . . . really sick and would take a while to get better. I didn't feel like I was exaggerating—my symptoms were that bad, my MRIs were that concerning, my AFP was pretty elevated—but I could feel myself lurching in the direction of the worst-case scenario every minute that I was awake.

"Let's just talk about what'll happen if I do die," I said to her. "What do you think people will say at my funeral?"

"Or we could talk about what'll happen when you live," she said.

Allison wasn't one for vague positivity. Her believing I was going to have a frightening surgery and be fine was based on her own experiences with frightening biopsies. I told her how obsessed with May 21 I'd become.

"One day you'll forget the date," she said. I didn't believe her.

"I never thought I'd forget the date of my first breast biopsy, but I have," she said. "I remember what it felt like to get diagnosed, but the when of it? I don't know anymore."

I couldn't tell if she was practicing radical acceptance or trying to spool me back to life. Either way, no matter how much I pulled up my tumor marker on her laptop, showed her how the graph was rising, I couldn't get her to agree that I was on death's door.

What I *could* get her to talk about was being useful, even when I was convinced I didn't have anything to give anyone.

"Babe, I haven't done anything for anyone in years," she said to me, when I told her how useless I felt.

All I saw was Allison doing things for people. She answered the phone when someone called looking for help with not picking up a drink. She answered the phone when someone called for help with a friend who'd been diagnosed with cancer. She answered the phone when her mother called, when her sister called. She answered the phone when I called, and she'd answered the doorbell every time I'd shown up, hungry for the love she could give me.

"I feel like all I can do right now is take," I said to her. People had been coming by. Visiting. Bringing me containers of turkey chili and books; my friend from the writing class took me to dinner at an Ethiopian restaurant around the corner; another friend came and sat in the back garden with me. I couldn't figure out why they were there—I had nothing wise to say to them. I had no money to contribute to the cost of the turkey chili, the Ethiopian dinner. I couldn't help anyone by writing about them; this time I really couldn't make anyone famous.

"I don't know if friendship really works like that," Allison said. "The thing is, it's really not about parity."

Parity was all I'd ever known about friendship. That a certain kind of score was kept. That reciprocity might not happen immediately, but that it needed to happen at some point: the invitation returned, the dinner bought, the phone call answered, the paper edited, the money sent. But I couldn't reciprocate. Definitely not now, and possibly not ever.

"I think maybe just let them love you?" Allison said after another friend had come, given me food and a book, and left. I told her I'd try.

And then, once again, Leila, ever reliable Leila, flew west and moved me from Allison's home back to my apartment, the apartment Cameron had now vacated, and rearranged the furniture to make it feel new—the sofa that remained, the television that remained—and took me to dinner at Chez Panisse, the relaxed upstairs café, of course.

My memories of this time are fluid, interlocking. Days stretching toward the surgery were endless, but too fast. I needed more time to prepare; I couldn't wait another second. I crossed days off the calendar, all heading toward Tuesday, May 21, that date I was so sure I'd never forget. There was only one thing on my calendar for that day: MOTHER-FUCKING BRAIN SURGERY.

Even though I felt like the most useless friend, people kept coming. Even though I believed that I might never be able to reciprocate, friendship kept happening, *to* me. Leila stayed with me for three days, pulling my apartment together, watching the diagnostic medical mystery series *House,* eating ice cream. Other friends came. So many called, so many texted, so many dropped by.

"Have you ever had surgery?"

I asked almost everyone I saw. I wanted to find the context. I wanted to know if I was doing this right. If Allison was right to try to calm me down. If I was right to panic.

As a child, I'd needed to understand where I stood in the world, whom I stood next to, and where my experience fit. There was always someone else who needed to give me permission—and that's what books did, and then that's what Allison did, and then that's what all of my friends did. What they still do. But before, in college, smoking after dinner in the eating club we both belonged to, a friend of mine said, aware of probably starting an argument and defending his position of reading only political nonfiction,

"Why would you waste your time with books that aren't strictly informative?"

I was apoplectic, using the same bravado that I used for years and years and years, arguing for reading memoir, fiction.

"But why, when there's so much out there to learn?" he said, and my response, my only response that I've ever really had, was that fiction, memoir, gives us a way of trying on moral selves. Later, in grad school, learning more about the role of internal moral selves and the ways that we can write ourselves into being, the power of narratives to be climbed aboard, the way in which correspondence and writing began to be ways in which humans organize themselves into moral people. Of course I read fiction, Allison's library of Cathleen Schine and Elizabeth Strout, and I also, in those four weeks between "we need to biopsy your brain" and seeing my name on the whiteboard, scheduled for a 12:20 p.m. operation, read memoir: Susan Gubar's *Memoir of a Debulked Woman,* Joshua Cody's *[Sic],* Barbara Ehrenreich's *Bright-Sided,* Emily Rapp Black's *The Still Point of the Turning World,* language after language after sentence spilling over me. I marveled at Susan Gubar's still being alive — how could she be alive after everything, after her insides had been removed, and this is where I learned the language of illness. Of debulking a tumor, for instance. Before, I had believed that tumors were discrete objects, perhaps tiny round balls of something, like eyeballs but made from tumor, easily removed. I didn't understand how tumors wrapped around vessels, into muscle parts, how they were made up of multiple forms. I read Suleika Jaouad's *New York Times* columns, and *Brain on Fire* by Susannah Cahalan, about anti-NMDA-receptor encephalitis, and Joan Didion's *Blue Nights,* about the illness and death of her daughter, Quintana Roo, and still I couldn't quite believe that *I* was sick, that this was happening to me, that I didn't have any choice or agency or moral involvement in the matter.

What I did have choice in was who I invited to touch my body. Not a medical touch; that was happening with my consent but mostly against my will. A personal touch.

I didn't know what would happen after the surgery, or how sexual I'd feel after having a bit of my brain scooped out. I also knew that my parents and stepparents had planned a caregiving round robin for the six weeks after brain surgery, which meant I'd have some kind of parental unit sleeping in my bedroom until the end of June. I was fresh out of my relationship with Cameron, but because I'd left this relationship on its own terms and not for someone else, I hadn't done the old Dorothy Parker thing of getting over someone by getting under someone else. My writing class flirting partner seemed less interested in actually sealing any kind of physical deal now that I was actually available, a trusty former fling turned out to have been coupled up for years, a college friend whom I propositioned after a dinner gently and kindly — but very firmly — turned me down.

I thought about heading to the surest thing I could think of: my ten-year college reunion. It was lore that everyone who hadn't coupled up immediately after college (or those who had and then gotten divorced) found each other at the tenth. It was where the freshly divorced new dads came to troll for graduates who'd spent their twenties traveling instead of getting married. It was where freshman-year hookups came to consummate more than a decade of desire. It was, I thought, my best chance. All it would have taken was a flight to New York, a train to New Jersey, and three days trying to find either an empty dorm room or a cab that would take me back and forth to a delightful New Jersey Turnpike motel. All I had to do was postpone my surgery by two weeks, get out there, get laid, get back, get scraped. It was a foolproof plan.

It's possible that anyone could have seen how . . . unrealistic . . . my plan was, which is why I didn't tell anyone. Except Allison. I was starting to get in the habit of telling just her everything. Days of us both homebound — her with the effects of cancer and its treatment; me with the aftereffects of a brain hemorrhage — made for languid hours of conversation.

"I just think it'll be a really good opportunity for me," I said to her.

I was perched on a chair in her kitchen, at the kitchen table where we'd eaten cheeseburgers I'd brought when she was sick and I was well. She was scratching her head, the hair starting to come out from this round of chemo. My shoulders were draped in one of her cashmere blankets, a blue one. My face was red from heat but my body was shivering. I was picking at a grilled ham and cheese she had made me.

"I want to go. I want to feel something else besides *this.*" She, more than anyone else, knew what *this* encompassed: the drumbeat of boredom and terror that underpins a *very* sick life.

"Well, the thing is," she said. She often started conversations by saying, "Well, the thing is." She also quoted others as always starting their observations with "Well, the thing is," even though I'd never heard anyone else ever say it. "The thing is, you're really sick right now."

"I'm feeling better."

"Babe."

I coughed. I could feel my eyelids sinking down. I was getting tired again. I'd been up for three hours.

"I think it'll be a really good distraction," I said.

"Do you really think you'll talk about anything besides your brain surgery?"

I imagined the flight east, the train I would have to take from New York to New Jersey, the way that I'd have to pretend to be okay with everyone getting as drunk as they used to get in college—Princeton reunions consume more alcohol per capita than even the Indy 500, an anecdote we all told each other, proud of ourselves — and I could feel the stamina that would take, and everything in me geared up to make it happen. I wanted to make it happen. I wanted to be able to take this trip and go and tell people I was getting brain surgery, or maybe not! Maybe I could be stoic and private and quiet and laugh about things and maybe by making this trip and having an awkward one-night stand in the computer room of my former eating club I could fix this. Maybe, if I tried hard enough to ignore reality, I could change it! Being in total denial had never worked before, but I'd never needed denial this badly.

"You're not well," Allison said.

It was the first time that I had to surrender. There would be other times, so many other times, but it was the first time that I realized that I couldn't out-think this, out-try this. I couldn't course-correct this. Almost everything else, except my alcoholism, I had been able to control. Allison knew that.

"I know you're used to being able to do what you want, but the thing is," she said, "sickness doesn't work like that.

"It just grabs you, and it beats you like a fish."

I wasn't used to Allison talking in violent terms, ever.

I started crying. Took another bite of grilled ham and cheese.

"I just really . . ."

"I know, babe."

So many of our conversations happened in fits and starts and in the acknowledgment of what we both knew. We both knew that she was dying. That I was suddenly very sick. We were finding our footing in these new roles. After I'd been living with her for a week or two, she turned to me.

"I'm so grateful for you, you know?"

I felt myself soften. I wanted to be someone she was grateful for. And then—

"I never thought it would be you. I mean, I always thought you were sort of okay, but . . . I'm surprised that it's *you,* who's here, who comforts me."

I was just as surprised. I had never been a person who comforted people. Seeing someone else's pain was terrifying. If I didn't know how to fix it, I didn't want to be with it. It had never occurred to me to go deeper into pain instead of immediately trying to pull someone out. To sit in the darkness, in the vast landscape that is the abyss of pain and fear and suffering that illness, or tragedy, brings. I had never done that before, but here, living with Allison, I started to.

That week, she got a CT scan. She brought the results home. She read the pages to me, over bowls of lentil soup. The text was dry. Just descriptions, as if from a textbook. A textbook written specifically for Allison's body, about her body. *Liver: innumerable tumors.* Innumerable. Literally too many to count. The rest of her body was precisely described. The tumors in her lung were measured, numbers of, and inches. The tumor near her bile duct, in inches. But in the liver? *Innumerable.* I pictured her liver, because the CT scan report didn't come with a picture, dotted with tumors. Couldn't they punch them out, or burn them? She'd mentioned an earlier ablation. *Good adrenals,* the report said, and we laughed because we had believed that I had adrenal fatigue, entirely possible, and so we thought about combining ourselves into one person.

"Together we're perfect," I said, and she knew that I meant it both as two puzzle pieces of body parts, and our friendship. It was also a way of holding on.

Allison did not want to die, and that's something that I often forgot. She had been sick for so long, been *terminal* for so long, that those around her, including me, became inured to it. It seems shocking now, utterly, that I could have become inured to her suffering, to a beloved's nearness to death. I think now about all the days I should have listened to her more. All the minutes I was distracted. All the times I forgot that she wasn't always going to be here.

Back to my distraction. I had to agree with Allison that I couldn't go east, so I turned my gaze closer to home. It became my singular mission to have sex. Just one more time before I went under the knife, before things changed. I wanted to feel that my body was something more than a subject of examination, of magnetic resonance imaging and CT scans and blood tests. The phrase "poked and prodded" comes up so much when we talk about testing, and yet the right word isn't "poked." A needle doesn't poke you. A needle, the kind of needle they need to give you so that you can get saline, or medicine, or contrast so that they can better visualize your brain, it's a wide-gauge needle, and they need to get it into the vein, and to get it into the vein they have to dig, sometimes. A needle that makes something go into your body is very, very different from the needle they use to draw blood, though that's something too, something that begins to wear over time.

For twenty-four hours in the hospital, I had blood taken every hour. Lying in my hospital bed, so confused that I was in a hospital bed, waiting for this to stop being this strange movie of my life and for everything to get back to normal, I heard the rattling of the phlebotomy cart, vials and vials and vials full of inky blood clanking against each other. I had never thought about my veins before, but those twenty-four hours started four years of thinking about them, learning about them. I learned that my right elbow crook was reliable until it was used so many times that it wasn't. And then my left. And then we went to my forearm, and then the phlebotomist went to my hand, to the tiny veins that spread across the top. My relationship with pain changed with those needles, and with that, so did my relationship with my body. I'd seen Allison talk about pain, seen her scoop four oxycodone pills into her mouth, swallowing with a sip of the Diet Coke that she loved, but I hadn't been able to imagine what it was like to feel pain every second. To feel a pain that increased and then decreased but never went away. To begin to feel the anticipation of pain as almost more painful than the physical sensation itself. Those twenty-four hourly blood draws set the stage for later draws, later IVs, for the way in which I began to live just on the edges of my body. The pain I experienced in the hospital was enough to knock out all memories of pleasure. Pleasure!

What did I think would happen if I had sex? Did I think I would be cured somehow? There was a part of me that believed that getting fucked would knock the sickness out of me. That I just needed a jolt, a rewiring in the other direction. I didn't know yet about pain pathways, the way that the body learns that the more pain a part produces, the more pain it will keep producing. Years later, my friend Lauren will tell me about the kindling effect of mental illness. That the more episodes a person has, the more episodes she's likely to have. This is how it was with my body. With my body and pain. And so I thought that sex could interrupt this trend, could create a new one. That my body could absorb and re-member pleasure and keep it, store it for later. For the later that I hoped so badly would come. Looking at my calen-dar, there was the day *after* MOTHERFUCKING BRAIN SURGERY. Would I see Wednesday, May 22, 2013?

I kept thinking about the one percent that my surgeon had mentioned. Why was I so afraid, when there was less than a one-in-a-hundred chance that something could go wrong? I couldn't see past my fear. But was this objectively scarier than a friend's knee surgery? Than my grandfather's quintuple bypass, which, sure, I'd registered, but not really? Why did I think that the brain was somehow so much more tragically dangerous than anything else? I did more research. Pan-creatic cancer killed almost immediately. Same with lung. Brain cancer, at least the kind of brain cancer that my sur-geon thought I might have, was actually treatable! Curable, even. And it wouldn't be pleasant, but it wasn't . . . the end of my life. So why was I trying to make deals with myself? Praying to some external force that the cyst might magically shift, reappearing in my elbow, my shoulder, my knee?

I had always been afraid of having my worldview changed. In college, I'd been drawn to drugs that heightened my exist-ing experience: Adderall, Ritalin, cocaine, alcohol. As much as alcohol was a depressant, it never changed my fundamen-tal understanding of the world. I'd taken ecstasy once and, wanting it to last longer, had smoked a LOT of pot. I'd hallucinated that the bathroom door was a swirling hydrangea made of nightingales, steeped in a millennial pink of God's love, and once the trip wore off I was terrified of ever having something like that happen again. Sometimes, when I was looking at a patterned floor, it would start to swirl. My mother, who admitted more and more about her early LSD use the older I got, talked about flashbacks like that. We hypothesized I'd accidentally dosed a hallucinogen. I hated the flashbacks. I hated anything that altered my filter, my perception of the world. Part of getting sober had been a rededication to experiencing everything *as it actually was*. I'd been in such alcohol-infused denial for so long that living in what I perceived as the real world was something I'd just begun to love. The prospect of brain damage, then, however implausible, however minute the chances, was what was so terrifying. It wasn't so much that I was afraid of treatment, or physical pain. It was that I was afraid of waking up different and not being able to notice.

And so I needed a familiar comfort. At dinner at a restaurant, after a meeting, after an hour I'd spent lying on the window seat because it was too hard to sit up, I announced to the table, six or seven or ten of us, the regular post-meeting group, what I was looking for: just sex. Probably just once. I knew I couldn't have a relationship, had nothing to offer anyone, didn't even have enough to offer myself. Every speck of love and compassion that I could find within myself I was turning toward Allison, who was getting radiation on her sternum; the cancer had metastasized to her bones. And so no Tinder, no OkCupid, nothing online; this had to be both subtler and much more straightforward.

"I have someone for you," a friend said. She had a steadiness, a measuredness to her.

"He'll be perfect," she said, handing her phone to me, a Facebook page open. I saw dark eyes, a chiseled chin, long hair.

I had always sought comfort in strangers, in the disappearing into another self that sex afforded me. At the time, I didn't think anything of seeking my deepest and most intimate solace from someone I had *never* met before — instead of turning to Leila, or any of my friends who were coming by, watching TV with me, bringing burritos that they paid for. I left Allison's house to go to the long-haired stranger's house. I left her house again to go to his house again. I chose to be with someone I'd never met before instead of being with her, lying with her, watching TV with her. The night before I went to see him the first time, I asked her what she thought about what I was doing.

"The thing is, you're looking for comfort," she said.

I saw the stranger once and then I saw him again, and again. Those nights became armor for me. The first night that I was with him, I hadn't been with a man for two years, and I remember standing in his room and looking at his body and then, as he moved, feeling his arms around mine and feeling his muscles flex and then feeling him grow harder against me and I said to myself, over and over and over again, *This is something different than terror, be here, and stay here, you are alive, here, now,* because I didn't know what was going to happen. I didn't know if this could be the last time I would feel anything besides fear, and then nothing.

I was scrambling for a foothold. Later, I would learn to find the foothold in my friends, and then even later, I would learn to find the foothold in myself, but here? Here I was desperate for a foothold from anything, from anywhere. From someone else's body, however briefly joining mine.

~

Two days before the surgery, I threw a brain-themed party: I served Jell-O set in brain-shaped molds I'd found online, tiny brain-shaped chocolates I'd ordered off of Amazon. I was hysterical with fear, and so I covered it up with adrenaline, with outward performance, with the dissemination of my worries, hoping that if I talked to enough people I could spread the terror around. I invited everyone I knew, and twenty or thirty people came, revolving groups of friends from grad school, from meetings, first in the park near my house and then back in my apartment once it got too hot to stay outside. We played Cards Against Humanity — I picked the card "a brain tumor" and got to use it every time. We ate cupcakes with bright green frosting, and a friend gave me a pair of argyle socks, and so many friends wrote cards, and my mother was there, because she had come in to be with me during the surgery and its immediate aftermath, and so was Matt, from the airport, who'd come with his girlfriend, and whose presence connected me to the person I had been before this had all started, a person I might once again be. Allison came, brought with her a box of doughnuts, brought Sadie back into the apartment, and even though I wasn't living with her anymore, something in our friendship had shifted, was shifting. I needed her, so much, and this time we both knew it.

The morning of surgery, awake, seeing the detritus of friendship strewn across my apartment: the cards, Allison's doughnut box, those argyle socks. No coffee. No water. Nothing by mouth. Jim, who I knew from the noon group where I'd met both Allison and Cameron, had offered to drive us, and we took the carpool lane over the bridge. As we crossed the bridge I looked to my right, to the icy blue water and the hills of Marin County. There was a part of me that was storing this up, trying to make a movie of my memories, and for what? I was trying to sear this vision into my memory because I thought this might be the last time I'd ever see it. That desire didn't make any sense, temporally — the surgery was scheduled for 12:20, and if I died that meant I'd only hold the memory for fewer than four hours. But it felt so vitally important to me to remember this, to remember this drive, the way the water looked, the sunlight.

This is the part where I want to say that I felt gratitude at the earth's beauty, the sun's shining beams glancing off the water, the kite surfers and windsurfers and so on, the boats, the cranes, the old bridge that wasn't yet the new bridge. I didn't. Instead, I felt a blank excitement — a guillotine of numbness falling over me. I had felt that numbness before, anytime someone had gotten too close to me. Anytime a boyfriend — Tim, or the writer, or Charles, because they all said this — had told me that I felt inaccessible, remote.

Someone was about to go into my head and take something out. Someone was about to come into my orbit, and do something to me, and say things to me, and change me forever.

∼

It was what I had always been the most frightened of.

act two

~

four

~

The morning after my brain surgery, I texted a friend.

ugh, dude, i've literally been brainwashed

The surgeon had draped my face, gone in through my right nostril, cracked the skull holding my sinus cavity together, reached around to the back of the pituitary, and drained the Rathke's cleft cyst he would immediately have recognized. As the scans had shown, the cyst had hemorrhaged into my brain, leaking blood and protein, infusing the architecture of the inside of my skull with error signals and faulty wiring; that's what the hallway fall had been about. And as my surgeon was able to see, it looked like it wasn't a tumor. After draining and sewing closed the cyst, he cleaned the area inside my skull with hydrogen peroxide.

When I woke up, I was high on Fentanyl and morphine and steroids and trauma. I was in a hospital bed in a room full of hospital beds, attached to wires and leads and IVs, and next to me sat a nurse whose sole job was to monitor my vitals. She handed me an ice pop, grape-flavored, and I took one lick before realizing how badly it hurt to swallow. She'd given me the ice pop to try to soothe my throat, which had been rubbed red and raw by a difficult intubation—only years later would I see, on a record I wasn't supposed to see, that I was extremely challenging to intubate—and I was so surprised by the ice pop that I lost my grip and dropped it down the side of the bed, and also my hands didn't work, and also it was hard to organize my body somehow. So she gave me another one, grape again. This one I held on to. It took effort.

My mother and Jim came in. They stood next to me.

"The surgeon's pretty sure the spot isn't cancer," Jim said. No one would be able to definitively confirm until the pathology results came back, but we guessed that the surgeon wouldn't have said he was pretty sure about something unless he was . . . *very* sure.

Jim texted the update to my friend Jason, whom I'd met in New York and reconnected with when we'd both, independently, moved to Berkeley, who had sat with me the day I'd found out I needed brain surgery, who had shown himself to be a steady and constant force in my life, whose friendship was becoming a quiet counterweight to my dramatic medical needs. We had bonded deeply during the fallout of my relationship with Cameron; I'd been ashamed of how that relationship had started, and ended, but Jason had listened compassionately to my every complaint, dodge, dissemble. We often had lunch together near campus, then walked through the eucalyptus groves and chatted about our lives, our families, our work. Sometimes we hiked in the hills of Mount Tam, looked at the water, made intimations of spiritual awareness. Jason had volunteered to handle the dissemination of whatever information might come from my surgery, a job I'd never have thought of but was so grateful he took, and one I remain forever willing to volunteer for myself. After Jim texted him the news, Jason had posted on my Facebook wall so anyone who was following the event could know what had happened.

I was glad for the update, but I had something important to ask. I just couldn't figure out how to ask it. *Could they check the stalk?* I tried to ask Jim and my mother, fighting the nausea and the aftereffects of my first round with general anesthesia. *Could they tell if there's cancer somewhere?* I was trying to find some certainty, to mark how I was supposed to feel. I remembered my surgeon telling me that the AFP was being produced either by the visualized mass or by this persistent pituitary stalk thickening. I didn't have the immediate diagnosis we'd all expected. The suspicious mass wasn't cancer. *But what can you tell me about the stalk?* I wanted to know so that I could know how to feel. If I should feel relieved, or even more scared; if the thickened stalk was producing the tumor marker, I was in even more trouble. I was trying to find a map, figure out the variables, the likelihoods, the possibilities.

There was a thin stick of dried blood coming out of my right nostril. I gently tugged on it, rolling my fingers on the edge of its crunchy hardness.

"Easy," the nurse said. "You can touch it, but *don't* pull on it."

It was a stalactite of blood that connected right up to my shattered skull. They'd glued the bones back together after they'd splintered them, but while it all healed back together, the blood stalactite was an essential part of the structural integrity of my brain, my head.

"If you start leaking clear fluid, go to the emergency room immediately." Right. Of course.

Feeling this blood stalactite, hearing that my cerebrospinal fluid could leak out of my nose, made me think of my head as a porous, shifting thing. I'd always thought of heads as sealed tight, like bowling balls. Nothing went in and nothing went out. I'd thought of the whole body that way; nothing ever *really* went inside. I'd spent years learning how to shield myself with an invisible wall that went all the way around me, and now, while I'd been asleep, challengingly intubated, I'd been profoundly penetrated. My skull had holes, breaks in the bones. My brain had a hole in it. Where *was* my brain? Where had the shattered bones gone? And how shattered had they been? Was my skull now held together with glued-together little shards? Or had there been a single crack? Had they used a drill? A hammer? A chisel?

While I was still figuring out the ice pop situation, the order to discharge me from post-op and transfer me to neurosurgery came in. I was transferred, attached to a heart monitor, and then left alone—my mother and Jim driving back across the bridge together, the nurses watching me from afar. I woke up to find a bag of pastries that a grad school friend had left, and I kept waking up and then wanting to stay awake, thinking that if I slept too much during the day I wouldn't sleep that night, but then a wave of pain would hit me. I remember a nurse coming in, handing me a paper cup with a single white pill. "Here, swallow this," a tiny white pill, and then, a few hours later, another tiny white pill. Every four hours, ten milligrams of OxyContin, time release.

And then four hours later. Maybe they just came in, or maybe I called them, asked for it, asked for two. I hurt. I had my phone with me, and during one of my awake periods, I found my phone in the sheets, forced my hands to work, and, after fifteen minutes of typing attempts, managed to post to Facebook, "Everything went well!! I'm alive!!!!"

And soon a friend wrote, "and already on Facebook!" but it wasn't that I was already on Facebook, it was that Facebook needed to be my first port of call. It was public and so it wasn't intimate. I had been so secretive for so long that the shock of difference felt like a soothing salve; sharing online was a way of outsourcing the unspeakable horror of what had just happened, of what I was still expecting would happen.

Posting to Facebook and watching the likes and comments appear made me feel like there *were* people who cared, hundreds of them; my problem was that I was stuck between believing the truth of all of that care and feeling resistance to the idea that showing up online mattered. My innate loneliness told me that it wasn't that hard to press "like" or write a comment about love and light. But the part of me that was so attuned to love that I could find it anywhere wasn't so skeptical. It did take effort. It did take thought. I read through the comments on my "I'm alive!!!!" post and saw how many people said how relieved they were, how they'd been thinking about me all morning. Friends had independently posted on my wall, some when this had all first started, some now. I was tagged in posts about luck and brain surgery. And it did land. This was real.

It's easy to be concerned about the ultimately disconnecting effects of social media, the internet. I remind myself sometimes, using what I've picked up as a historian, that part of the human condition is to be panicked about our current technology, to believe that we are on some kind of unsurvivable brink. In the nineteenth century, travelers believed that the speed of a train, a brand-new technology, would irreparably damage their brains. I hold on to that historical fact when I think about how distracted we can seem now, and how many books there are about how bad social media is. But here, I *felt* how social media connected me, particularly to people I might not have been close enough to put on my email list, but who cared, for real. I received messages of support and love from people I hadn't seen or spoken to or sometimes even thought of in ten or twelve years. Was that support not supposed to count because it had come over the airwaves of the internet? It counted to me.

The downside was subtler, but also more insidious. Social media, and particularly Facebook, with its emphasis on stories and narratives that appear on a timeline, forced my experience to appear to have some form of consistency. Scrolling through my own page, my own timeline, I could see *a story* beginning to unfold. Something had happened; I'd posted a picture of the first ER, and then of myself from the hospital, and then I'd gone quieter, posted links to articles, and then I'd posted about brain surgery, and then I'd posted after brain surgery. The story that social media was telling was that an awful thing had happened but now it was over. And that was the limitation. I couldn't express the day-to-day, minute-to-minute changes.

No matter how many selfies I posted, no matter how many comments I responded to, I couldn't use social media to describe that day in the hospital when I tried to reckon with the loss of a significant percentage of my brain; or the nights, later, when I checked my email (always from a DONOTREPLY@ email address, the ultimate brush-off) to see the results of my latest blood test, could see the graph of my tumor marker steadily rising. As much as social media gave me a platform to ask for (and receive) attention, I couldn't use Facebook posts to work through what I ended up working through with Allison: the logics of grief, the great expense of living in the kingdom of illness, the deep belief that I should be doing this differently, that I was being sick all wrong. Facebook was a powerful platform but a limited one. It connected me to people as long as I could be the subject of a trackable and followable story; the problem was that here, for the first time, the edges of my experience had become too messy to hold.

～

When we'd booked the surgery, my family had booked plane tickets. The plan was that my mother would stay for two weeks, then my stepfather Alex would come, then Julia, my father's wife, whom he'd married a few years after he and Leila had broken up, and then my father. A friend whose husband had gone through six brain surgeries brought me a wedge pillow, knowing that I couldn't lie flat for six weeks. I also couldn't sneeze, bend down and put my head below my shoulders, or blow my nose for six weeks.

This emphasis on six weeks made me believe that in six weeks everything would be better and different and most of all fine, and what I didn't know, what I couldn't have known, was that all of this was just the very beginning of the very beginning.

The day after brain surgery, a friend organized a group of alcoholics to come and sit in my living room, and I sat in a chair leaning my head against the wall while we went around the room, each person talking about how she stayed sober today. And then it was my turn. All I could talk about was the pain, the indescribable pain. Much has been made of the indescribability of pain, of illness being its own Sontagian kingdom, of the impossibility of truly regarding and understanding the pain of others. I tried, and yet all that could come out was

"This is a pain unlike anything I have ever experienced," and

"This is a pain that will end my world," and

"This is a pain that I would do anything to have removed," and

"Oh my god you guys this hurts *so* much," and it is then that I realized why doctors prescribe opioid painkillers after surgery.

Of course I didn't want to take opioids. I'd been sober for almost six years, and even though my drug of choice had always been uppers I was scared of what painkillers could lead to. I had heard enough horror stories—of someone sober twenty-six years who had surgery and took opioids and died an alcoholic death on the streets. My fears always led to that: dying an alcoholic death on the streets. If someone looked at me the wrong way, if someone criticized me, if I received a work rejection, or a romantic rejection, my brain, without even slowing down long enough for me to catch it, went there. It was only when I stopped and asked myself, *And then what? And then what? And then what?* that I realized that this is where every fear led me. Drunk, alone, dead.

That morning, if someone had offered me heroin, which I'd never tried, and told me that there was a one percent chance that it would take this pain away, I would have done it. I would have put it into my eyeballs, or through my ears. I would have put heroin up my nose, through the blood stalactite, which I would have pulled on, if someone had told me there was a one percent chance that it would ameliorate this pain. I sent my mother to the pharmacy, immediately.

As much as my friends—a rotating group made up of people from meetings and grad school—were present, as much love as they showed me, I still felt closer to Allison than I could to anyone else. I was in her world. Even though I didn't have cancer, having had such a dramatic surgery, I'd crossed into her kingdom. Allison and I had developed a new lingo, one I couldn't share with my well friends, only because they'd never experienced what I was experiencing. They were still saying to me the things I'd learned not to say to her. That everything was going to be fine. That I looked great. That they'd heard a story about someone who'd had cancer, and right, they'd died, and it had been awful, and wait, why had they brought up this story? I tried to remember to translate everything everyone did into *I love you. I'm so sorry you're in pain.* Because that's what the soup deliveries, the magazine readings, the friends sitting by my bedside and telling me their dating stories were communicating: *I love you. You matter. I'm so sorry this is happening.*

All I'd ever wanted was to know that I was valued, that I

was loved, and here was evidence, hour after hour, knocking on my door, pulling up a chair, smiling. *I love you. I'll see you soon.*

~

The first night that I was home, as I lay down to sleep in my bed and listened to my mother lie down in a twin bed across the room from me, as I wedged myself right onto the pillow, I started thinking to myself about what the *after* of all of this might be like. I understood, finally, that being the star of a PhD program or being the favorite of the professors or being the person who didn't fit into the cohort because she had published, that none of those things would save me. That as much comfort as achieving had given me up until this point, I had finally reached the end of the line.

It was ironic that my mother, whom I'd blamed for so much of my loneliness and drive, was the person who'd come to see me through this. We'd become close, in the way that we were both capable of, after she left Vishaan and became a hotshot visiting professor in New York City. For a while, we both lived in New York; I was still drinking, so it was hard for me to connect with anyone. But once I got sober, I pushed through the discomfort I felt about what I perceived as her discomfort. One warm spring morning, over a year since I'd gotten sober, I made amends to her in an Indian restaurant in Curry Hill.

I listed my wrongs. I'd asked for money for health insurance and spent it on drugs. I'd made minimal effort to ask her about her own life and her own interests. I'd been self-centered and rude, and I told her that I'd often treated her as an ATM, without offering much of myself in return. During a process of inventory, I'd come to see that much of my loneliness, and many of my resentments, started with me. That I always expected the other person to go first, to open up before I would. I'd never gone first. I'd never told a secret, hoping that someone else would then feel a safe permission to tell hers. Telling my mother the things I had done that I wasn't proud of was the first step in developing a closer relationship; I didn't know if she'd want to get that close, but I knew I had to try.

She'd been skeptical about my sobriety. My family is big on drinking, after all, and everyone manages to both enjoy their martinis and hold down good jobs.

"Have you thought about moderating?" she asked, meaning well.

"Maybe try a desensitization approach?" That day I told her that it had been more than alcohol.

"What were you into?" she asked.

"If you really want to know, I'll tell you," I said.

That hour was the most honest conversation we'd ever had. She asked about what drugs I'd done, and why. I told her about how captive I'd felt to tiny bags of white powder, about the number of times I'd tried to stop and couldn't. I told her about the sheer relentlessness of addiction, how my brain told me, every day, to change my mind about deciding to stop, that I could always stop if it got *really* bad. She didn't say much. She paid the check. I told her I'd pay her back the money she'd lent me; it would have to be in small increments, but I would do it.

That afternoon, she called me.

"I had no idea it was so hard," she said.

"You are so brave," she said.

"You are so strong," she said.

Since then, I'd come to appreciate what I'd always judged. Her intelligence. Her grace with male colleagues who tried to trip her up. The way in which she could hold a lecture hall's or seminar group's attention by talking about moral theory and Epicurean ethics. Her manners. The way in which she'd embraced me, even though my life was so far from what she'd imagined. Sometimes, I could tell that she wanted to be warm, had to break through decades of her own sheltering, her own discomfort with intimacy. Our relationship was a chance for me to try something different, to try to go first.

It's often said that tragedy brings families together. In one way, my illness brought my mother and me closer than we'd ever been. But in another way, I like to think that we were both ready to be this close; we just needed a little deus ex machina to give us the permission.

Lying there, thinking about my post-surgery life, I knew what I wanted to believe in. What I wanted to live for. It was people coming to visit, who came because they loved me, for reasons beyond my comprehension. Who came to be next to me even if there was absolutely nothing that I could do for them, and this, this was the crux of it all.

Of course I'd needed help before, and I'd received it. Like when Leila had taken me in, or when Allison had unconditionally loved me when I hadn't known I'd needed it. But this was different. This time, I didn't have the luxury anymore of pretending that I could be fine on my own, of dis-appearing from a friendship when the relationship became too intimate. I didn't have time to believe that one day, even-tually, I would figure out how to be loved. I had to just ac-cept it.

~

In the days after brain surgery, people from the noon group where I'd met Allison came through. Allison herself came through. She was on a break from chemotherapy, and so this was something new, her coming to visit me, her feeling stronger than I was. She sat by my bed, held Sadie in her lap.

"How's your body feeling?" she asked. No one else had asked me how my body felt. They'd been more interested in distracting me, or of telling me stories about their own sur-geries (so many secret surgeries, I found out, which made me wonder if the whole world was full of people burying their medical experiences, if this was normal, if I was just making a big deal about mine). I knew I could tell Allison the truth.

"It hurts, so much."

She reached her hand out and touched my arm, the same way I'd touched hers so many years earlier.

"I know, babe. Rest if you can."

I knew rest might be useful, but I wasn't really convinced it was necessary. My body had always recovered. I'd always been able to bounce back, move through. Because I was so consumed with the need to produce and perform and do a good job and be a star, I'd lived with a fundamental discon-nect between my actual body and my controlled experience of my body. My body was failing and falling apart and I had learned that I could always push it just one more inch. One more day. One more performance.

But something did happen. Five days after surgery I started vomiting and didn't stop. First I was vomiting smoothie, and bite of doughnut, and spoonful of chickpea salad, and then I was vomiting water, and then I was vomiting bile. I threw up and then there was relief, an instant, a second, and I got back in bed and then it started again. I called the number I'd been given on my discharge sheet. I got a call back within twenty minutes.

"This is Dr. Gardner. You're vomiting constantly? Go to the Emergency Department. Now."

I waited for three hours in the emergency waiting room, my mother there with me. Every three minutes I went to the waiting room bathroom and threw up, the tiny sip of water I'd taken, the remnants of a pill. I was sweating. I was hot. The nausea was beyond anything I'd ever imagined, and as an alcoholic I'd experienced a lot of nausea. This was next level. I was desperate for relief, so desperate that even if I wasn't throwing up on my own I still walked into the bathroom, locked the door, and stuck my left index finger down the back of my throat.

The nausea became my whole world. I could not imagine a time in which I hadn't felt like this, or a time in which I wouldn't feel like this. I felt a deep intuition that if we couldn't get this nausea to end, *I* needed to end. For the first time in my life, I understood the desire to die. For the first time, I understood that living could be more painful than dying. Allison had talked to me about her husband's last days, as he died from lung cancer.

"It wasn't the pain that was the worst," she'd told me. "It was the nausea."

She'd told me that she'd held corn chips to his mouth, letting him lick off the salt, hoping the sodium might help. I thought about her now. About licking a corn chip. I needed this feeling to end. It would never end.

I was admitted; they gave me some IV Zofran for nausea and morphine for the pain. I stopped vomiting. I equalized. My electrolytes were normal; I had enough sodium. That's what they were concerned about—a loss of sodium. Low sodium is what had been so awful for Allison's husband.

"But get it checked on Tuesday," the doctor said as she discharged me and so two days later, on a Tuesday, I went with my mother and got it checked.

I was sure it was still fine because I felt fine. I felt calm. Calmer than I'd felt in as long as I could remember. I wasn't vomiting anymore. I did feel like I couldn't fit into my clothes, but I'd probably gained weight from the doughnuts. I'd gone for a walk the day before—a walk!—to the park, with someone who'd come to visit me, someone I didn't know that well but who was joining the ranks of rotating visitors, coming for her own reasons or maybe just kindness, I couldn't tell—I didn't need to know, it was enough that people were coming. We walked to the park at the end of my block and we sat down on a stone wall and I tried to have a normal conversation, to ask her about her life, and everything felt like I was reaching, grasping, trying too hard.

"How's work?" I asked, and she answered but I couldn't understand or absorb the answer. Nothing was making sense, but I didn't want to tell her that.

The next day, I was still calm during the blood draw,

which found that my sodium was 122. *Critical low.* At around 120, the brain begins to shut down. Sometimes permanently.

For all of my pre-surgery terror, I hadn't considered that I'd *actually* die. Now it was suddenly extremely possible.

"You have to get to the hospital—*now,*" the doctor said.

They called for the ambulance, and the paramedics arrived, and I was friendly, and cordial, and all of this was happening very slowly and very calmly. I was surprisingly calm with all of this, just noticing how strange it was, that I was being ambulanced over to UCSF for, I heard, "direct admit to the neurosurgical floor," and then my mother said to the paramedics as they strapped me in, put an oxygen tube up my nose,

"Don't pay attention to how she's acting; she's very, very, very sick."

When I heard her say that, I understood, on an even deeper level than when I'd heard that number, that this was serious. My mother had been calm and informed since the minute she'd landed. Seeing her worried sparked something in me. Still, my conscious mind wasn't worried. I watched myself wave to the nurses who'd seen me in. Being chipper with the paramedics. Roll my eyes at how dramatic this all was.

"Don't be fooled," my mother said to the paramedics. "She's very scared."

I didn't feel scared. I knew I should feel scared. But I didn't. This felt like some kind of game. Like I was watching myself. *Look at me on a gurney / look at me being wheeled down the halls of the clinic / look at me in the parking lot / the ambulance / look at me with oxygen / look at me now.* As we drove over the Bay Bridge, I lay on the gurney and looked out the back window at the highway receding into the distance, at the towers rising, at the cars behind me.

Even though I was calm, I was also starting to think that I might be dying. *How ironic,* I thought. *From a complication no one even warned me about.* For all my feverish Googling of brain cancer mortality rates, I'd never once searched for "brain surgery side effects" or "brain surgery complications." Riding in the ambulance, I could see my mother's face. She looked worried. She held my hand. She asked the drivers if they were sure about where they were going. Fear was starting to edge into my consciousness, a lace around the edges, barely perceptible. I oscillated between terror and peace. In a way, my pre-surgery fear was coming true: something was so damaged in my brain that I couldn't quite figure out who I was or what was important. I remembered reading about people feeling extraordinarily calm before they died. Was this that? When I'd thought about that kind of pre-death calm, I hadn't imagined it would actually feel like this. My acceptance felt real. True. Earned. And so I thought, but still calmly, about how San Francisco's high-rises might be the last landscape I ever saw. Just as I had with the water on the way to brain surgery, I tried to remember the view, save it for later, for the end, even if the end was less than an hour away. I was surprised to see that I didn't feel upset that I was going to die. I was just curious. Bemused. I hadn't thought I would die like this, not for years, and suddenly it was here. This was how I was going to go? How strange. How surprising. And like this? Looking at San Francisco traffic? It felt so unusual, all of it, and yet I accepted it.

I scrolled through the futures I'd held for myself. A future in which I was married. A future in which I had children. A future in which I owned a dark wood dining table and finally, finally threw that dinner party I'd been fantasizing about. A future in which I figured out how to bake a Momofuku Milk Bar birthday cake. A future in which I finally bought a couch. A future in which there were infinite more books to read and infinite more movies to watch. A future in which I existed. A future in which I was loved. A future in which I could feel it.

~

"We have a direct admit to Neurosurgery."

The ambulance pulled into the Emergency Department driveway. I was rolled out, transferred from the ambulance gurney to a hospital one. And then: corridors, lights, my mother walking next to me. And then the eighth floor, Neurosurgery, the one I'd just left last week. My name written on the board again, and my medical record number, and the names of my surgeon, Anand, and my pituitary specialist, Smith. I was wheeled into a room that overlooked the park, the de Young Museum swirling upward. I had given a presentation at the de Young not that long before. I had gone and put on a dress and walked around with a bunch of graduate students and lectured about the building, about its porous sheath. I had pointed to an Andy Goldsworthy project, a crack that let the darkness up, that brought the light down.

The resident came in twenty minutes after I was settled into my room, handed me a tiny paper cup with one tiny blue pill almost lost in its folds.

"This is Tolvaptan," she said. "It should reset your sodium."

I swallowed the pill, so easy, so tiny. And then I wasn't allowed to drink. Nothing. And then I started to pee. Every thirty minutes my bladder filled again, even though I wasn't drinking. They measured everything that came out of me, and then the night nurse came in, and time, time was so fast and yet so slow, and nothing happened but everyone was busy, and I posted on Facebook that I'd been hospitalized on the top of the hill, if anyone wanted to come, and did anyone come? So many did. My friend who'd lent me the wedge pillow came, and my friend from college and grad school came and ate chicken nuggets while I watched and sucked on another grape ice pop, and a friend from the noon meeting came and brought me *US Weekly* magazines and talked to me about her relationship while I lay back to close my eyes, then fell asleep while she talked, and my mother, who had gone home the night before, came back the next morning and brought my computer and I stayed there for two nights and I lost eight liters of water, eleven pounds. My body shrank back to how it had looked, and the attending came in, and he said,

"Oh, this happens — the pituitary can get irritated and just tell your body to hold on to water, and that's how your sodium gets so low."

It was a common complication. My mother, ever interested, researched the situation — postsurgical hyponatremia, and found articles from the eighties that mentioned ten-day hospital days after brain surgery. They'd sent me home the morning after, less than twenty-four hours after they had shattered my skull and glued me back together, and was this the new era of medicine or the new era of cost control?

No matter: after two nights in the hospital, everything equalized, and then I went home.

~

While the drug helped my body in the moment, and while the pathology confirmed that the mass had been a cyst, we still didn't know what was going on with my thickened pituitary stalk.

"When we see a thickened pituitary stalk, we watch it for a few years, and then the tumor just . . . pops up!" Dr. Anand had said.

I kept hearing his voice, his particular phraseology. Before the surgery, I'd Googled him three or four times a day, watched the videos he'd posted to YouTube about his minimally invasive spinal surgery. I didn't think this was a variant of Stockholm syndrome, where a hostage over-relates to her captor, though that was an obvious joke. It was more that I wanted to feel as though we had some kind of relationship. This man existed in space. I existed in space. But we would come together only through my silence, through his putting his hand inside my skull. The few sentences he'd said became a line for me to follow, a way of trying to connect. "Slam dunk," "pops up," "we just wait," "we just watch." I let his phrases spill over me, trying to let them wash away the uncertainty. But uncertainty was all I had. The ground shifted every moment.

The plan was to check my tumor marker every three months, MRI every six, and just wait. "Try and keep yourself busy in the meantime!" Dr. Smith said, cheerily. I had a hard time keeping myself busy with anything besides figuring out how to kill time before the next test. The middle ground felt like a new torture. I'd survived brain surgery, hooray! I didn't have cancer where we thought I would, hooray! But then, whisper voice: *I might still have brain cancer, just not where we thought.* It was becoming clear that mine wasn't a story with a clear trajectory. This wasn't a cancer story I was used to, or a cancer story I had ever heard. And after a while of trying to explain where things stood and why more wasn't happening, I started to feel like I couldn't communicate the details, because there weren't really any new ones, besides we didn't know but we were worried, and my tumor marker kept rising, but not enough to do anything, and I kept feeling awful. I didn't know how to explain, so I didn't. I didn't know how to react to the well-meaning faces of disbelief.

"You mean you're just going to *wait?*" friend after friend said to me. I was given doctors to call, referrals to cross-check with. I sought a second opinion at Stanford, where the doctor told me the same thing as my UCSF neurologist had: "Let's just wait, see what happens." The further I drifted into the ether, the less communicative I became. One by one, piece of information by piece of information, I stopped posting so much detail online, started storing it inside my body instead. *Slam dunk* in the right pocket of my gallbladder. *Pops up* into my left rib cage. *We just wait* into the very middle of my back.

Even more confusing was that I was one hundred percent compliant with my post-surgery instructions, and still I wasn't recovering. For all my worry, I couldn't prevent the fact that I *did* turn out to be one of the one percent with complications, not a sinus infection but something else, something more insidious, harder to catch—an irritated pituitary that couldn't right itself. Damaged, my brain stopped being able to control water, to keep water, and so I was desperately dehydrated and always drinking water. I wondered what else had been affected. I knew that my usual sharpness was gone, but I couldn't access the memory of having been sharp. A condition of my brain damage was the lack of ability to process exactly *how* my brain had been damaged. I knew this is what I'd been afraid of, but it was, in a perfect Möbius strip of a loop, just enough of a shift that I couldn't register the change. I'd been afraid of getting brain damage and not figuring out how bad it was; once it happened, I still couldn't really tell.

It took more than six months for my brain to even begin to physically right itself. (It would take years for my faculties to fully return.) Six months of two to three times weekly infusions of saline, which was the only thing that could get me rehydrated. Six months of trying, trying, trying to get back to things—like rescheduling my qualifying exams for my PhD program, which I was still hanging on to, or going to my support groups, or telling myself that I couldn't read anything more taxing than *US Weekly* because I was tired, not because my brain would never snap back to how it had been.

More important, though, it was six months of being too physically strung out to be able to worry about whether I was worthy of love. And so it was six months of deepening friendship. Of talking to Allison, of slow walks with Jason, of visitor after visitor after visitor coming by. For those six months, I was almost never alone. I was starting to learn that even though I *was* the only one pressed up against the edges of this experience, the only one who read hundreds of PubMed articles about occult intracranial germ cell tumors, the only one who tried to read my own online MRI images to see if I could find something the radiologist had missed, it didn't mean that no one could be next to me. As solitary as those (often) nighttime excursions were, during the days I almost always had company. Friends came to my house. Friends brought me books. Friends read to me. Friends watched *How I Met Your Mother* with me. Friends explained the finer plot points, reminded me of the cliffhanger of the episode we'd just watched, which my brain had already forgotten. Friends hugged me when I cried. Friends lay down with me when I fell to the floor with shame and horror. Friends ran out of meetings with me, put their arms around me, and told me how sorry they were that this was happening. They held me.

～

My phone, always, and from so many:

> can I come by?

> what are you doing tomorrow want a visitor?

> hey I'm in your neighborhood I'm gonna stop by I have candy

～

The second week of July, Allison and I took a field trip to J.Crew. We both needed new clothes, were sick of wearing sweatpants and hospital gowns. I was feeling a little better. She was feeling a little better. And so, the mall! And me, back in the saddle of trying to find some distraction. I was thinking of joining Tinder. I figured it could be as loose and casual as I needed it to be. I was obviously not in the market for a real relationship. I told Allison my plans and also my worries; I might have been moderately delusional about my readiness to date, even casually, but at least, I tried to show, I was moderately *aware* of my delusions.

"I guess I should figure out how to be less intense about my situation," I said, as if I'd just come up with the thought. "I don't want to scare anyone away."

I figured she'd take the bait and say something like I wasn't that intense and I was doing just great and I couldn't possibly scare anyone away anyway because I was a very relaxed and enjoyable person to be around.

We pulled up to a stoplight. A long one. She turned to me.

"Well, babe, the thing is . . . you're a pretty acquired taste. And you're really not for everyone."

WHAT?

"You're a funny girl," she said. "You *are* really intense."

I opened my mouth to protest this intimation of intensity. To say that maybe I wasn't as intense as she thought, or of course I was super intense, because I was going through a super intense thing, but normally I was totally chill and relaxed and not even remotely a little bit intense, or like how could she tell me I was an acquired taste when I'd just been through the greatest trauma of my life, and maybe she could be a touch gentler with me. But I gave up before I even started because of course Allison knew me better than I knew myself, would have known that none of this was true. I'd never outright lied to her before; there was no reason to start now.

"You're just not for everyone," she said. "But there *is* someone who you're going to be absolutely *perfect* for."

"Once I tone it down a bit, you mean." I was feeling a little bruised.

"No," she said. "I mean that there's going to be someone who's going to find it really easy to love you, just like I do."

"Okay, once I stop being so much . . . *myself*."

"No. Babe. No. The things you think are bad, those are the things that make you lovable."

She knew all the things I didn't like about myself. We went over a few of them. I was talkative, enthusiastic, bossy. I overshared. I expected too much of people. I was less focused than I felt I should be. I was self-centered and selfish and forgetful and didn't listen all the time, and if I wasn't interested in a conversation I didn't even pretend to be interested. I was terrible at small talk; I went deep way too fast. I sometimes lacked boundaries: personal, physical, sexual. I came on way too strong and then disappeared way too suddenly. I was secretive. I never wrote thank-you notes. I was easily distracted. I was jealous of my wealthy friends. I didn't particularly like to do anything that didn't feel easy. I was competitive. I was short-tempered and impatient. I should say, to all of the above, I *am*.

Allison knew all of that. I wanted to disappear into the seat. I thought about picking up my phone again, pretending to need to send a text. But time with her was precious, and I'd finally figured that out.

"I guess I'm glad you didn't sugarcoat this?" I said, after she'd finished confirming that my worst fears about myself were true.

"Your flaws aren't the point," she said. "The point is that these are all the things that make you *you,* and I love *you,* and so will someone else."

None of this felt remotely possible. I itched to change the subject. But before I could, she spoke again.

"Trust me," she said. "I'm flawed too—and it was just so *easy* for William to love me. You don't have to tie yourself up in knots to try to be someone else. And besides, you're not very good at it."

I looked at her.

"You're so good at being *Eva,*" she said. "Why don't you just go with that?"

I'd never thought that I could just . . . hew to my own mean. I thought about Allison. She also talked a lot; sometimes she gossiped. I'd heard her say uncharitable things; she'd said them about me! For as much as I idolized her, I was also deeply aware of her flaws. (The list was much the same as mine.)

Was it possible that someone could love me the way I loved her? The way she loved me?

"Okay, okay," I said, barely conceding. "I'll believe you when it happens."

Two weeks later, it did.

five

~

It was a Thursday night. The day marked six years since
I'd had a drink, so I went to a meeting. A friend wanted
me to celebrate afterward; I demurred, but he insisted he
buy me a doughnut. My loyalty to doughnuts was unswerv-
ing, so I agreed, and he bought me a doughnut, three actually, and then he asked me how things were going, and I
said I'd been kinda sleeping around, trying to have as much
fun as I could, and did he know any good candidates for a
one-night stand, and he asked if I liked tall, handsome, brilliant physicists, and I said whatever, and he called his friend
Winston, who was apparently a tall, handsome, brilliant
physicist. Some back-and-forth and it was agreed: Winston
would come by in half an hour or an hour, and we would
meet, and see what happened.

And so I met my husband. We shook hands. He sat down.
He congratulated me on six years. It was his thirtieth birthday, incidentally. He'd planned to go home to eat cake but
he'd decided to come by instead, for some reason. We talked
about *Star Trek* and juicing and traveling through South-

east Asia and Scotland (him) and Europe (me). We talked about my PhD program, about my work on the midcentury modernist architect Eero Saarinen and his wife, Aline. We talked about where I'd grown up and where he'd grown up, about his parents' Stanford connection and how my grandfather had gone to Berkeley at fifteen. We talked about storage units and apartments in Orinda, about his job working for a Japanese technology company, about how he was looking to get a full-time physics-related position but it was tough, about how once I'd worked as a sandwich artist for Subway. He told me that he saw sound waves and electromagnetic waves everywhere. He asked me more about my work, my writing. I told him about living in New York City, about traveling for years to look at buildings in Switzerland, Washington, Moscow. I told him about living in Canada and about how I had a brother who sold rare books. I told him about my mother. I told him about my father.

He came home with me. He came to bed with me. And still we talked, the whole night, the entire night, until it was 5:45 and he had to leave, right then, to make it home in time to get ready for an early-morning work meeting. I slept for a few hours, but I couldn't really fall asleep, not after this.

"You're gorgeous," he had said to me at two or maybe at three, as I reached over him to get a glass of water. We kept trying to go to sleep but we couldn't; every time we remembered that the other was there we had to touch each other again. Of course we had sex. I heard in my head a refrain, from the text I read to help me stay sober: *I don't know what this is you've got, but you'd better hang on to it.* I felt myself press my face into his chest and feel the warmth of his body and the power of his body and I knew: *I don't know what this is I've got, but I'd better hang on to it.*

Did you notice that we never talked about my illness, not once? It was the first time in six months that I wasn't a patient, a number, something on a chart. I was myself, I was Eva, a long-forgotten Eva, the *Eva* that Allison was talking about, a person who had been so blindsided and so terrified by everything that was happening that I'd forgotten that I had interests, that I liked television and books, that I traveled, that I had ideas. My conversations had for so long revolved around what had happened to me and what might happen to me that I had forgotten that underneath the tumor markers and complete blood counts and scan results, I was a person.

I called Julia, my stepmother, the one my father had married after he and Leila split up.

"I met someone," I said. I tried to describe him, tried to describe what had happened, but I couldn't. I didn't need to.

"You sound more like yourself than you have in years," she said.

It is easy to fall in love with someone because of how they make you feel about yourself. And that was part of it, of course. But I also discovered, as we spent days and days and nights together, nights when we didn't sleep and it didn't matter, that I loved him. That there was something in his ease and in his kindness and in his unequivocal knowledge of who he was that I wanted to protect, that I wanted to celebrate. I loved him for more than how he made me feel about myself. But I was also, because of all that had come before, able to believe that he loved me. Not for who I might become. For who I already was. The more I woke up with him, the more we began to see just how well we fit, just how perfectly we were matched, the more I heard Allison's voice in my head. *I love you, and so will someone else.*

I didn't mention how sick I was that first night, but I did tell him, and quickly. The second or third night we were together, I mentioned a doctor's appointment.

"I want to understand more," he said, and so I turned the light on, sat up in bed.

"I have a tiny thing in my brain that might be cancer," I said. I saw no point in dissembling. "We aren't sure, but I'm being tracked."

He didn't say anything.

"If you want to stop this now, I understand," I said. I did understand. I didn't want him to be with me out of some sense of obligation, out of feeling like he had to stick it out because he'd started something. For all I knew he'd thought this was a fling (we both knew it wasn't).

"I'd rather you peace out now as opposed to later, but I'll understand either way," I said. "Basically, things are probably going to get weird at some point, but I don't know when, or how that weird will look."

"I'll stick this out," he said. "I can do weird."

And so we were together. Of course things were going to get weird. Things always get weird when two people decide to try to merge their lives. I didn't know yet that my weird of having a maybe-brain tumor would soon be matched by his weird of needing a *lot* of alone time and loving to play video games. We put my being sick in the same category as his hatred of doing dishes, or mine of doing laundry: a fact of life that, sure, was inconvenient and annoying sometimes, but that didn't fundamentally change who we were. In a way, we started at the end — in sickness, rather than in health, with the bad stuff as well as the good — and so everything that came after was weighted equally. I had to go to the emergency room a lot, but also I liked to go to the grocery store. He tended to be very thorough in his scientific explanations, but was also fine with our not knowing how much time we had together.

Winston never became my caretaker. Our relationship became a place of refuge from the pain and terror and mundane numbness of the everyday medical horror that shaped the contours of my life. The first time I went to the emergency room after we'd started seeing each other, a few weeks after we'd first met, I agonized over whether I should tell him.

"Would his knowing make any difference?" my friend who'd driven me asked.

It wouldn't. There was no reason for him to worry, and there was also so much reason for me to protect what we both knew by then was love from the infringing power of the narrative of love and caregiver-ness. As the weeks turned into months and it was clear he really wasn't going anywhere, I began to invite him to more medical things — like an early-morning spinal tap, which we turned into a romantic city getaway the night before — but Winston never occupied center stage of the support army. I think that's why we are still married. I think that's why our love was able to have its own rhythm. Yes, some things were accelerated, but

Winston was a bulwark against my anxieties, my fears. He was compassionate, and he was loving, but my body was not the centerpiece of our relationship. My whole self was.

~

A few months into being lovestruck, I was deep into the waiting game. Both my neurosurgeon and my pituitary doctor were interested in keeping a close eye on my brain.

"We'll MRI again in July," they said in May, and in July, when not much had changed but the stalk was still thick, "We'll MRI again in January."

My tumor marker was tested every month, and it kept rising. The medical literature suggested that a thickened pituitary stalk plus an elevated AFP level, which my blood showed, plus a plethora of neurological symptoms, which I experienced, all indicated an intracranial germ cell tumor. We'd initially thought the AFP was being produced by the lesion, mass, whatever, wedged between the cleft of my pituitary. It wasn't, but it could be this other thing. Or not. We weren't sure. The only thing we were moderately sure of was that now, suddenly, I had a little more time before the tumor Dr. Anand expected to "pop up" appeared.

What to do with that time? I spent much of it with Winston. Much of it with Allison. I wanted to make the most of this time, because I believed that I hadn't swerved away from my suffering, but had merely prolonged my wait for it. Into that in-between swept my friends, the indivisible and ever-shifting group of people who loved me, the sum of the whole so much greater than its parts. I expected them to disappear once the initial surgery aftermath was over, but that isn't what happened. Instead, they kept texting.

hey what are you doing can i come over tomorrow

hey do you want to watch an episode

hey i'm in your neighborhood can i stop by?

And then it was December, a month until my next MRI. Winston and I moved in together and realized that his need for alone time dovetailed perfectly with my devotion to Allison. We agreed that every Friday night and every Monday night I would sleep over at her house. She was going through another round of chemotherapy, an attempt to keep the ever-metastasizing breast cancer at bay, and she needed more help, more company than before. We put my stays on her calendar as "slumber," which was supposed to be short for "slumber party" but was also, I knew in her poet ways, a reference to the ways in which our time together was still dreamlike, out of the world. Now that I wasn't with Cameron I wasn't constantly texting someone when I was with Allison. I was *with* her, in the time of no-time, in the in-between, in the time of waiting, me for a diagnosis and her for a final death sentence, the real one this time.

One of those nights, a few weeks after she started radiation on top of the chemotherapy, as we lay in her bed, after dinner but before the ice cream — coffee and chocolate for her, a sliver of a spoonful of vanilla Rice Dream for Sadie,

a pint of something absurdly high-maintenance for me—
I showed Allison a line graph of my tumor marker. It was
a steadily rising line, starting in February, when we'd first
measured it, and ending now, December.

"I don't know why they're not doing more," I said to her.
"I just want to know—I just want to know either way."

The closer I got to the next piece of information, the more
I felt I needed to prepare myself for the onslaught of pain I
imagined was coming. Facing an MRI that I'd waited eleven
months for and that was around the corner now was like finally being near a bathroom after hours on the train and realizing you can't hold it for even one more minute.

"Trust me, babe," she said. "You don't want it to be cancer."

"I feel like at least then I'll know."

"No," she said. "It's *never* good news when it's cancer."

Was I picking up a note of defensiveness? The infringing
on her territory I'd done before was even more at the fore-
front now. I told everyone I knew that I had maybe-can-
cer, probably-cancer, that I probably most likely had brain
cancer but we had to wait until January for certainty. This
month of waiting for that confirmation was starting to feel
interminable. I was also seriously stepping on her diagnostic toes.

"Babe, if they were worried, they would have acted by
now," she said.

"I think they've just forgotten me," I said.

"If they thought that you were going to die of this, they
would scoop you up, and they would put you on an ocean
liner of medical help, and they would take care of you.
That's what happens when you have cancer."

We were the only two people who could understand each

other—two women, both dealing with cancer, or at least with the cancer world—but there was also, within the collective space of our shared experience, this unbridgeable divide between us. She *was* dying. I just believed that I might, and sooner than I would have liked. Time with Allison gave me the space to be able to say all the things I felt like I shouldn't say to my friends, to the people who were supporting me, but it also reminded me about how alone I was in my specific experience. She was someone who understood why a CT scan is scarier the fourth time than it is the first, why reading blood work results obsessively at night on your phone while you're supposed to be watching *Girls* is somehow soothing, how sometimes a negative result can be more surprising and destabilizing than one that requires immediate action. But she was also someone who had an answer, who knew exactly what was going on.

"I could never go through what you're going through," she said. "But it's just not the same as having cancer."

∿

"We have a freedom, living on this side," Allison said to me once, after I joined her in the kingdom of the ill, as we sat together in her car, driving to Whole Foods and then to her house, Sadie on a blanket on my lap. She stopped the car, pulled to the side of the road, turned to me. This was important enough for her to stop driving.

"The thing is," she said, "it's very, very, very expensive."

There was a freedom. Things that I had cared so deeply about didn't matter anymore. The fourteenth time I was on a gurney waiting for the saline to kick in was the first time

I didn't care that it was a Tuesday or a Thursday, a day on which otherwise I would have made myself try to be productive. My grad school cohorts were surpassing me, passing their exams, publishing papers, presenting at conferences. It was, for the first time, okay that I wasn't the biggest star. (I wasn't even on the radar.) I was starting to take pleasure in the tiniest of things: in a Momofuku cake a friend had sent from Portland via New York, a box of bath powder that came in beautiful packaging from a friend traveling through Europe; finding a T-shirt that said ZERO FUCKS GIVEN and wearing it to a doctor appointment, under a sweater, of course. I felt myself leaning into these moments of freedom, of laughter. I watched The Lonely Island music videos and when there was a truly funny scene, I laughed, and as I laughed I felt my body move, felt the laughter move its way through my brain and into my bones, and I stopped myself and put my hand on my chest and felt my chest rise and fall, rise and fall, and I knew that I was alive.

The night before my January MRI, a group of friends came over, and we posed in a photo like the Baby-Sitters Club, leaning against each other, our faces lit up with purposefully overdone smiles. I was tense. They were tense. But we laughed as best we could. We posted the photo on Facebook because we posted everything on Facebook. And the next day, I went to UCSF and walked through the parking lot and into the tunnels where the radiology center was, and I went into the machine and then back out, and then a few days later I went to see my pituitary doctor and he said something like,

"Yeah, looks kinda the same as last time. I think you're good for a year." And then all of 2014 lay before me and it felt that nothing would ever be wrong again, but nothing would ever be okay again, either.

I had not expected this. I shared the news, immediately. I received responses, immediately:

> You must be so relieved

> Thank God, I've been praying for you

> I'm so glad to hear this

> You must be so relieved

> You must be so relieved

> You must be so relieved

I was not relieved; I was baffled. Whiplashed. In the months leading up to the scan, I had tried to anticipate every outcome, by which I mean the worst outcomes. I had thought about what it might be like to go through chemotherapy, had mentally prepared myself to go through radiation on my brain. I'd prepared for, if nothing else, an answer. For the next step. For something to *do*. For something to be done. But here, I just had another year — another year of waiting, and living in limbo, and wondering if maybe *next* year would be the year that everything would change. I'd heard about "scanxiety," the way in which living a life that is parceled out into between-scan increments never fully lets us relax, the way that a memory of an awful test can take hold, can become all that matters.

I thought about Allison and the way I watched her anxiety around scans only increase. How I'd watched friends of mine who'd maybe had a suspicious mammogram once get more and more nervous as their annual checkup came closer. As nonsensical as it would have seemed to me before I got sick, I felt that it was harder to live in the in-between than with even the most devastating certainty. That space of not-knowing felt infinitely harder to deal with than the world-wrenching pain I had anticipated.

In other words, I had armored myself up so much that instead of feeling relief, or joy, or whatever I thought I was supposed to feel, I was just numb.

But then there were my friends, still showing up.

hey you around?

i have something for you

can i stop by?

six

~

I posted the news of the results on Facebook. So many of my friends commented. I was starting to learn that Facebook wasn't a performance of friendship; it was a central element. I couldn't really go anywhere, but I could participate in my relationships by commenting, liking, responding to comments, picking up hashtags and running with them. By performing inside jokes for each other and for anyone else who might care to join. My friends and I inched our intimacies forward through hashtags, photos, quotes. It wasn't what I'd thought: that friendship existed in one place and was performed in another. It was that all of this — posts, memes, hashtags — became part of a dance of intimacy and connection. The performance wasn't a representation so much as it was its own iteration. And so rather than lamenting the onslaught of technology or the falseness of the internet, I felt like the pictures we all posted and commented on, the hashtags we came up with, were doing incredibly deep work for all of us. They became threads of friendship and connection, unspooling forward.

∼

My brain was fine, for the next year, but there was some concern about my fluctuating heart rate, which was being caused by either my pituitary or something more systemic. My doctor suggested I have a cardiological workup to rule out something called POTS — postural orthostatic tachycardia syndrome. And so I went in for a tilt table test, and they started with an EKG and then suddenly it was the attending, not the resident, who came up to me.

"Has anyone ever mentioned Wolff-Parkinson-White to you?" he asked.

Someone in some emergency room had thought I might in fact have this congenital heart defect, but I thought we'd ruled it out. I told him as much.

"Nope. You have it. Definitely."

I was strapped to a gurney that was about to tilt up.

"What do we do about it?"

"You'll need an ablation," he said. "Make an appointment for a consult to talk about it."

He wouldn't tell me anything else. I went through the tilt table test and I was negative for POTS. It was just my pituitary, still healing.

∼

I went in for a consult.

"Has anyone in your family experienced sudden death?" he asked.

I thought it was a weird way of asking if someone had suddenly died, but his website had listed his areas of expertise and "sudden death" was one of them; apparently it is a known medical category. My paternal grandfather had died very suddenly of a heart attack, I said, but other than that, everyone had died rather slowly, of non-heart-related causes.

"You have an extra pathway in your heart," he explained. "Any episode of tachycardia — fast heart rate — could lead to that pathway catching and then not slowing down . . . which . . . well . . . then . . . ."

He didn't have to say "sudden death" again. I knew that's what he was talking about. I thought back to every time I'd felt my heart flutter, every time it felt like a grinding gear-shift caught in my chest, every time I'd done too many lines of blow and felt my heart race. He explained the ablation to me.

"We thread a wire through your groin and up into your heart, and then we burn that extra pathway."

I asked about the risks of surgery.

"Well, the risks of *not* doing surgery are much higher."

My good and bad pathways were close together; he said there was a small chance I'd end up with a pacemaker.

"But we'll be extra careful," he said.

(Me, internally: *As opposed to the other, non-careful heart surgery option?*)

Any idea I'd had that I could go through this by myself had been completely destroyed by my brain surgery experience.

"Of course you need company," Allison told me when I told her I was asking for help.

But I didn't even have to ask. People texted me from the beginning. *Can I help?* and *What do you need?* and *Anything I can do?* started lighting up my screen.

So much help was coming, and I wanted to accept it, and Allison was trying to teach me how to accept it, and how to ask for it even if it wasn't landing on my doorstep, and still I had to fight shame: that I had something else, something new. Once again, my story didn't make sense; I didn't know how to explain it. I thought that I owed my friends some narrative completion, a consistency of experience. That we had all, somehow, invested in a particular trajectory, that to swerve would be wrong. I believed that we had all gotten on board my probably having brain cancer and my probably dying soon, and now I wasn't probably dying of brain cancer but had this heart condition that could kill me, and I felt the onslaught of pressure, pressure I'd picked up not from what anyone said but the subtler forces of our cultural narratives, the repetition of illness-related stories that make sense. From the idea that tragedy starts at point A and has only two possible outcomes. My experience was different; it started at point A, then went to point A.5, then swerved to Point X, although point A was still a through-line. I felt like needing a different kind of help would mark me somehow: as not tough enough, as too desperate. But I also knew that I needed a different kind of help with heart surgery than I'd needed with brain. I was more tired. I was more scared. I knew more about what happened to a body after surgery, about how slowly mine tended to recover. I had a deeper understanding of physical pain, and of the emotional confusion that comes with this kind of experience.

"Are you going to be okay?" an old friend asked. I felt my heart quicken, my voice rise.

"Oh, you're asking me because I'm psychic?"

I was ungraceful. I was undignified. That's what desperation produces. And the kind of help I needed was of the abstract variety, a kind of permission to do this however I was going to do it. Moral support. Total acceptance. And that's the help I'd never before known how to ask for.

It was less about who was going to go where, the logistics of presence and companionship that can take over these tragedies. I'd seen families struggle with not having been there during the moment it all ended; the belief that some of my friends held on to that they had failed me because they hadn't physically been there during my hospitalization or surgery. But what I needed wasn't only someone to sit next to me, though I did need that. I needed people to tell me that it was okay not to be brave. That I didn't have to believe in myself or my inherent strength. I so desperately wanted to do the right thing, but no one could give me directions. I felt like a scout, forging ahead to scope out a landscape none of us had ever been to, returning to tell the story of what it was like, here at the edge of the abyss.

Allison told me that I was being brave. I didn't think so, not really. I thought being brave meant being stoic and making jokes and laughing and never crying, and I was making jokes and laughing but I was also posting videos of myself crying and losing my shit in public, and I was constantly talking about my heart surgery, and everyone could see my terror, or so I thought.

"It's brave to show that you can be scared," she said. "It's the hardest thing in the world to ask for help."

But am I doing a good job?

"Yes," she always said, every time I asked her. "You are."

∽

The night before heart surgery I invited a group of people to see a movie. Because of the possibility of waking up with a pacemaker, a.k.a. bionic, I thought there was nothing better to do than go see the *RoboCop* reboot. Plus, Allison and I had developed a serious Joel Kinnaman obsession, and even though she couldn't come, I felt it my duty to . . . appreciate him on her behalf. I have a picture from that night, and half of the people who came are people I would be happy to see if I saw again but am not in daily contact with, and half are people who have become part of the fabric of my world, and that began to be the pattern. People were showing up and disappearing and showing up again and disappearing again, and instead of my resenting those who disappeared, I learned this: When it comes to illness, individuals become exhausted. The group, though? That larger collective, made up of ever-shifting parts? It's inexhaustible.

The procedure itself was so smooth—as was the recovery, no complications—that I wondered why I had been so terrified for the four weeks leading up to it. A few days before surgery, after I'd posted something about how worried and nervous I was, I'd gotten into a Facebook spat with someone who had tried to comfort me by telling me I'd be fine, that it was just a procedure, that it wasn't even a surgery. But I didn't want to minimize this. I didn't want to make myself feel better by hearing about people who'd had this procedure and then gotten on a plane the next day. I didn't want to be inspired by a rhetoric of toughness. Too much of our culture tells us not to make big deals of things, to quietly lick our wounds, to retreat. It also tells us to be brave warriors, to show fearlessness in the face of terror. But I wasn't fearless. I wanted to lick my wounds in public. I wanted people to be with me and see how afraid I was and say, "Yes, it's terrifying." I wanted to sink into the fear I felt instead of skipping ahead to the part where I'd be okay. And in the end I was okay, or at least my heart was.

I thought about that month that I'd spent experiencing moments of paralysis, terrified to move in case my heart caught fire, of baking recipe after recipe out of the *Momofuku Milk Bar* cookbook just to give my mind something to do besides Googling Wolff-Parkinson-White. Of collapsing to the ground after a meeting. I had a brief flash of wanting to go back in time, to do it all over again. To be stoic this time. Not to cry so much. To do a better job being brave. But then I remembered Allison. *It's the hardest thing in the world to ask for help.* It was. And I'd done it. By going through this surgery, I'd thought I might learn something about the particular architecture of my heart. And I did, but not in the way expected: What I learned from having a tiny strip of my heart burned off was that I don't have to know what the help looks like to deserve it. I don't have to be numb to be brave.

∽

I spent my recovery period studying for my PhD program's qualifying exams, writing out notes on massive pieces of poster board with which I covered my living room walls. I studied Ralph Waldo Emerson's letters to Margaret Fuller; James Joyce's letters to Nora. I studied the history of the letter, and the post office, and while I was doing that, my friends and I continued to perform our friendship in text and on Facebook. It was our own contemporary version of Twain's letters home, of Emerson's long and meandering approaches to Fuller. I was learning about the history of life writing in nineteenth- and twentieth-century America, and I was also conscious of how deeply ingrained that practice was becoming in me — of experiencing something and then writing about it. I remembered something a friend in New York had said, that people who grew up before the internet always decry children and young adults today, saying that they never write anymore because they're always on their phones.

"But that's exactly true — and they're writing," my friend observed.

The constancy of texts and Facebook and then Instagram hashtags that my group of friends and I were engaging in were as deep and intimate as Emerson and Fuller's letters, or as eighteenth-century private diaries.

I took my exams — three hours of oral questioning from five examiners — and passed. The hours that I spent talking about ideas, history, buildings, and material culture were a marker of my return to another life, my older life. But my approach was different. Instead of seeing these exams as a necessary marker of my finally being smart enough, I was truly satisfied just to be able to go. To speak sentences. To string thoughts together. To recall facts, and names, and dates. To feel, sentence by sentence, that my brain was recovering.

At home, Winston and I had moved past having the usual

fights that people who move in together for the first time have. About how much time we would spend together. About what time we went to bed. About who did the dishes and who did the cooking. About what we were going to do about money, or who got to pick what we watched, or if we really needed to go to the farmers' market *together*. What had started as six months of passion had morphed into something calm, easy, everyday. We were the fabric of each other's lives, the backdrop from which everything grew. He called me every day from work and we talked about the latest experiments he was running, or a work meeting he'd had, or about a particularly difficult student of mine, or, sometimes, a test result I'd received. And he came home every day at five thirty, walked in the door, took his headphones out of his ears, and came over to kiss me where I sat at the dining table we'd used to eat on exactly once before I'd co-opted it as my desk, covered it in a morass of papers and notes scratched on the back of receipts, medical bills, and envelopes. I am an inveterate hoarder of paper records, of objects that remind me that I exist, and so I had kept every discharge paperwork, every ER account, every doctor's slip.

As we continued to twine our lives around each other, I remembered what Allison had taught me about parity. That relationships aren't built on a process of reciprocity, but of love, and affection. If I'd had to keep score, I would have failed; I couldn't give Winston all that much besides my being alive, but I did my best with that. I scratched his back and head while we lay on the couch watching *Doctor Who*. When he called with a work problem, I talked it through with him. I went to the farmers' market every Sunday that

I felt well enough to do so, and cooked dinner as often as I could. Winston's culinary enthusiasm was matched only by his creativity: he wanted to add mustard to everything, cook the radish garnish, add some crushed shallots to his morning juice. I dealt with the logistics of our lives; my experience dealing with inordinately complex health-related paperwork honed my skills with leases, taxes, the amount of organization it takes to keep a household running. I listened to him talk for hours about nanotech space elevators, gave him space and silence when he needed it. But beyond the catalogue of moderately useful things I did, I just *was*. Early on, I'd told him that I might not be able to have children. That if this was something he really wanted, he should rethink this relationship.

"I don't need to have children," he'd said. "What I need is to be with you."

I was able to hear that because of the way Allison had loved me. He just needed me. He just loved me. And there I was.

A few months after the tilt table test, I was able to absorb my own water. I still drank a mix of electrolytes every so often, just to help my body along, but the constant crisis had waned. We still didn't know what was going on with my brain, but we knew that we had a year—and a year was long enough for me to get far enough away from one appointment and then far enough away from the next that there was a whole middle space into which I could open a life. I felt like I was wedging myself in between two crisis points and then opening up, like an umbrella, or a flower, forcing myself—my interests, my personality, my desires and things I thought were funny—into what had previously been this tiny interstitial space. My health no longer became the sole topic of conversation whenever I met someone, old or new. Instead, I had space and time and compassion for my friendships. The people who had rallied around me, the army that had showed up, I started being able to listen to their problems more. Actually, I started having friendships where problems weren't even part of it—we just had fun.

Even as I got stronger, my friends kept up the same rhythm of visits.

The question came up, sometimes explicitly, about why my friends were spending so much time helping me. And the question makes sense if we see friendship as a system of debts and credits. If a phone call must be answered, if like must receive like.

In all of the literature about friendship, in all of the advice columns and podcasts and essays and posts about how to be a good friend, I rarely come across its most fundamental point, the one that I learned during these years, over and over again. That friendship, true friendship, is often just about two (or more) people who love each other. The details, which are often extravagant, are just the details.

~

As I got better, Allison started to get sicker. Our Friday nights were still happening, as were our Monday-night sleepovers, but as we emerged from winter, she started to talk about her head hurting. I still had head pain from the brain surgery, and she'd often said how grateful she was that she didn't have that — that her pain was terrible, but it wasn't in her head. The opioids clouded her thinking.

"God, someone like me, who lives with words, to be so foggy all the time, it's the worst," she would say, but her thinking wasn't clouded by pain. And now, suddenly, she was talking about the inside of her head.

"Do you ever feel like you have to put your hand in front of one eye so that you can see?" she asked me one winter night. She turned to me. She was bald, for the first time since I'd known her. She was going through yet another round of chemotherapy to try to deal with these innumerable liver tumors. She hadn't gone bald quickly — her hair was there one day, and then it thinned, and then, weeks later, she shaved it. I looked at her head. She had a beautifully shaped head.

"Also, everyone tells me I have a beautifully shaped head and I just — I don't want to be bald! I don't care if my head is beautiful!" she said.

I was glad I hadn't opened my mouth.

She was reclining in bed, holding one hand in front of her eye, looking at the TV screen. I looked down at her pillow, covered with tiny black hairs. Her hair grew in between chemotherapy appointments — every three weeks — and then it fell out again when the Taxotere reached peak immune system effects. Her pillows were constantly getting covered in the tiny little hairs that grew, the debris that her body was making.

"Fast-growing cells," she said to me. "That's what chemo kills: Fast. Growing. Cells."

She pointed to her head.

"Hair: fast-growing cells." I knew that. But then also—

"Lips, fast-growing cells; fingernails, fast-growing cells; the inside of your *mouth* —fast-growing cells."

A bottle of something called Magic Mouthwash appeared in her refrigerator, and it started replacing the mashed potatoes and bowls of ice cream I was used to seeing her eat.

"What does it do?" I asked her.

"I don't know," she said. "They give it to all the chemotherapy patients whose mouths are being ripped open on the inside."

It seemed like something was changing for her. As much as I'd seen her go through chemotherapy and radiation, I'd never seen her go through a cycle of chemotherapy like this. Because I was staying with her on Friday nights, I'd seen her on lots of chemo days. But this time the result wasn't a steroid high and lots of chatter. This time it was something different; she asked me to put her friends' numbers in my phone in case I had to call them to take her to the emergency room (I didn't have a driver's license; I was functionally useless). I slept in the back bedroom but always offered to sleep with her, which is how I learned that she and her late husband had slept separately every night of their marriage. She preferred to sleep alone, and so I went to the back bedroom, but I left the door open. I didn't sleep well those nights. I was waiting for something— a cry, a yell, a sob. Sometimes I tried to go to sleep and couldn't, got up to get a glass of water. She'd hear me and yell, "Heyyyyyy!," and I'd crawl back into bed with her and we'd start up *Girls* again, or maybe *The Mindy Project,* which she also loved and which was still new. Sometimes she tried to get me to watch a French film, but I always turned her down.

We shared a Hulu account for a while. It was my account; I just gave her my password. Just recently, looking for something to watch, I scrolled through my watchlist. It was all stuff that made sense—*Mindy, Parks and Recreation, New Girl*—and then suddenly it was Godard films, experimental Hungarian movies, documentaries about disappearing wildlife. It took me a minute to register that this was all stuff Allison had put on and never watched. Eighty-one titles in total, a list of things she had meant to get to. Movies she might have watched with me, if I had wanted to. I have only been able to scroll as far as six or seven movies. Any farther, and she begins to unfurl before me. Any farther in, and I will remember too much, too many nights that I turned down her choices, too many times that I picked the movie. Any farther in and I will not survive the grief.

I've told Winston never to touch the watchlist. I've told him we will never cancel Hulu. It is one thread that continues to tie me to her, and I will never let it go.

A few days after the midway point of her chemo, she called me, left a message. "The chemo is working like a *dream,*" she said. I was on campus, heading into the clinic. I'd gone in for a checkup. I called her back. "I'm so happy," I said. I knew that's what I was supposed to say. And part of me was happy. And part of me was tired. Tired of her dying. Tired of the roller coaster, of starting and stopping a treatment, of starting another one, of it working, of it not. I knew that there was no way she'd be cured, that she would only suffer more. And so what would this dreamlike chemotherapy give her?

It gave her a few more months.

At the beginning of April, she got an explanation for the headaches. Her cancer had metastasized to her brain. It wasn't brain cancer; it was breast cancer in her brain, a distinction that I would never have known about until I had to read everything I did for myself. She showed me the diagnostic printout. There, in bold type, written with total neutrality: *life expectancy: four to six weeks.* For two years I'd been waiting for cancer to take over my brain. But now it had taken over hers.

I started coming over more frequently. I brought the books I needed to read for school. Or I tried to read them. She distracted me every time, by asking me what I was reading, or telling me what she was reading.

"Oh, I *love* Nabokov," she said when I told her I was reading *Speak, Memory*.

"Oh god, I can't *stand* Roth," when I told her I was reading *Exit Ghost*.

Friends of hers would come to take her out for a walk with Sadie, and it took her an entire hour to get out the door. Small things were becoming difficult: putting on her shoes, getting the leash. She wanted to bring two tote bags full of books, her wallet, papers, her medications, all for a walk around the block. I had to stop myself from getting irritated, from telling her it would be fine if she left her stuff at home. I had learned that needs don't always need to make sense to be real.

❧

And then she couldn't take Sadie for walks anymore.

❧

And then she couldn't easily get out of bed.

❧

And then she started waking up in the middle of the night.

❧

One night I woke to find her standing by my door, naked, leaning on her cane.

"Is someone in here? Who's back here?" she said. She'd flung my bedroom door open. I got out of bed, went to her, held her.

"It's me, it's okay, it's Eva. Let's go back to bed?" An instant later she was back to herself again:

"Oh god, babe, I'm so sorry to frighten you." And then, "I'm having a hard time keeping track of what's going on."

I woke one night to find her standing in the kitchen, talking about the Kennedys.

She heard me step into the kitchen. Stopped what she was doing. Looked down at herself. She'd hooked a skirt over her arm, thinking it was a shirt.

"Oh god, I have no idea why I'm out here talking about the Kennedys," she said. "It just seemed really important."

Watching her flit between the Allison I'd known and this different Allison, one whose brain was being shoved aside, invaded, removed, was the most devastating—and loving—relationship I'd ever experienced. I realized, following her lead, that my job was not to try to fix what was happening, or to help her feel any other way than she did. My job was just to see her. To comfort her. To love her. Just as she had seen, comforted, loved me.

A Friday night:

"Did you know that time doesn't work the way we think it does?" she said to me. "It's all mixed up, actually," she said.

"Are the men in the basement still there?" she asked. Her basement was unfinished, had been empty for twenty-five years.

"Where are all the girls who came with you?" she asked. I'd arrived alone.

"Who's sleeping in the back right now?" she asked. No one. One night, Sadie escaped into the backyard and we forgot about her for an hour.

And then, "Is Sadie in the other time now? Did you know there are two Sadies?"

Frantic at the thought of having lost Sadie, I checked the back door. There she was, perched patiently on the back step. Allison had let her out an hour earlier and had forgotten her. Allison never forgot Sadie. Allison was never seen without Sadie. Allison brought Sadie to chemotherapy, to all of her appointments, to her CT scans.

"Yes I AM a service dog!" Allison liked to say as she placed Sadie's service vest—worn only in restaurants or chemo suites or other places dogs were strictly not allowed—over her tiny body. Forgetting me was something that I could rationalize. Forgetting Sadie? This was the end.

A few months after her diagnosis, it was time for a home care nurse. It was also time for me to go to Germany, for a long-planned trip with Alex, who had remained a father to me, and my brother and Winston.

In Germany, Winston and I got engaged. We'd talked about it before, and so there was no proposal, no surprise. He asked Alex to have breakfast, put on a tie, asked for his blessing, and then we were engaged. The simplest of moves with the happiest of outcomes.

Before I left for Germany, I visited Allison. I climbed into bed with her. I held her hand, and stroked her arm, and I lay with her and we watched TV, like we always had. When I left, I leaned over the bed and held her, kissed her on the cheek and felt the softness of her skin, smelled the lotion she put on her face to keep it from cracking. I smelled the antiseptic scent of her Magic Mouthwash, the detergent she used for her cashmere, the sweet smell of the dried apricots she loved.

"I love you," I said to her.

"Oh, I know, babe," she said. "I love you too."

And then we sat, our arms entwined, holding each other loosely, easily, as we always had.

When I came back a month later, she was still alive, living out her days on a hospital bed in her main room, accompanied twenty-four hours a day by a home care nurse. She lived longer than any of us had expected. And her brain faded even more, her sharpness finally gone. The home care nurse broke open little pellets of methadone, sprinkled them onto pudding, onto applesauce.

"She's *still* hungry," the nurse said. We — her friends — were all amazed. But I didn't want to see her like this; I didn't know what to say. She was there and not there. Sometimes we made eye contact and I could see her, in there, terrified. And sometimes she looked at me with a blank confusion.

In the last weeks of her life she rediscovered how much she loved the Beatles, and as one visitor came and replaced another, the Beatles kept playing in the background. I came by once and saw a woman from the noon group sitting next to Allison's bed, holding her hand, singing along with "Let It Be." I couldn't sing. I was younger than Allison by decades; the Beatles didn't matter to me the way they did to her. I wished I could just sing with her like everyone else was. But I sat next to Allison, and held her hand, and tried to tell her about our engagement, our wedding plans. I showed her a picture, taken on my phone, of the wedding dress I had tried on and decided to buy immediately. I showed her a picture of a complicated cake, taken on my phone, that I had baked the week before.

Mostly I tried to show her how much I loved her, how much she had meant to me. There was a day where I could see her, the Allison I'd known, the Allison who'd walked me through so much. She was here, with me.

"What is it, babe?" she said. I held her arm.

I'd tried so hard not to make her death be about me. Had tried not to say that I'd miss her. But I couldn't keep it together anymore. I couldn't hide what I felt from her.

"I'm going to miss you so much," I said.

"I know," she said. She held my forearm, and I hers. I felt the softness of her skin.

"I'm going to miss you too," she said. "I really am."

I let myself finally cry, the way I'd wanted to when I'd first found out she was dying. Instead of trying to be strong for her, I took all the permission she'd ever given me not to be brave, and I looked *at* her, past the face that had been rearranged from chemo, past the baldness, past the hospital bed.

"I love you so much," I said.

"I know, I know, I *know*," she said. "I love you too. I'm so sad. I'm so sorry."

She was there. I could feel it. And then she retreated.

Allison taught me what it *felt* like to be loved. She set the template, reset my wiring. Because of who she was, her love was able to gently break apart decades of fear. Allison midwifed me into being the person I had always wanted to be. She loved me so consistently and so completely that I had no choice but to finally see what had always been there: that the world is not full of anger and darkness and pain and rejection; rather, that all of those things exist, yes, but shot through at every point with love. I had known how to love others, but I had never known how to accept it myself. Allison taught me how to be loved.

~

She died while I was out of town. I was with friends, who showed me the same kind of love she had: open, accepting, present with what is in front of us. They kept me distracted so that I would not scream myself to death. They kept me safe in the words and thoughts and questions that they asked, in the waterfall of love and distraction they poured over me. That was love. That was a love that had always been there. And that was what Allison had taught me to see.

What I learned from Allison's death was that stories don't end when we're ready, but when it's time. I had prepared for Allison's death for the five years that I'd known her, and yet when she died I was not ready. She died even though I desperately did not want her to.

Her death destroyed me, left a hole in my body and my brain and my heart, a different kind of hole than surgeons' scalpels and wires had made, a hole that would never heal. Her death was not narratively necessary; it did not and will not teach me anything. It was her life that had.

Before she died, she asked me about her life. What I saw from it. If she had been valuable. She hadn't ever had a particularly interesting job, and although she had written poetry, she'd never published any. She was a good wife; a good stepmother; she was a friend to so many others in the same way she was a friend to me.

"You've changed my life forever," I said to her. I think about it now, the tiny chains, her role at the center of so many lives, even lives that will never know more about her than what I might say about my friend Allison. She changed my life, and her kindness seeps through me now, her words lodged within my synapses, ready to be heard by someone else. I had never before quantified a life in terms of its effects on others; Allison's was the deepest, richest, most valuable life I had ever known.

~

A few months after she died, I had my last brain scan.

"I couldn't tell you what happened, but everything's back to the way it should be," my doctor said.

Did he think I needed another MRI?

"I mean, maybe, if you want, you could get one in three years? But I dunno—yeah, I think you're okay!"

So what had happened?

"I don't really know," he said. "Maybe when the cyst ruptured it caused some inflammation on the stalk?"

That would have explained the post-surgical pituitary dysfunction, and the weirdness (not a technical term) on the MRIs. And my tumor marker, the other piece of the puzzle, had, after precipitously rising for the previous year, leveled off at a manageably abnormal level. It hadn't risen in months.

"Have you seen this before?" I asked, unnerved by his casualness and also lack of precision; we were dealing with issues where, I'd learned, a millimeter could mean a literal lifetime of difference.

"Sometimes these things just happen," he said. "But yeah, nothing exciting in your head—beside your brain, I guess!"

I accepted his answer. It was easier than mustering myself for another fight, for asking for more details. And I wanted to be okay. I wanted to be done with the Neurological Surgery clinic. I wanted never to go to that eighth floor again. And so, a handshake, and then a celebratory handstand outside the clinic, and I was done. The brain stuff was over. I had made it. I was okay. My doctors had been slam-dunk sure that I'd had indolent brain cancer but . . . I hadn't. I wished I could have told Allison that I was okay. That she didn't need to worry about me anymore. That, surprise, it looked like I would live, probably for a long time, or at least I now had the same chance as basically anyone else. Returning to this world would take some time, but I could do it. I wanted to do it. I wanted to care about things besides tumor markers and brain MRIs and the tiny moments of joy and happiness and friendship that I so hungrily sought from those around me, from those who loved me. I wanted to come back.

And so Winston and I planned a wedding, this time with an expanded sense of the time we would spend together on this planet. We invited a hundred and twenty people, and they all came, drove up a winding mountain road. A friend read one of Allison's poems, one that ended with the line:

> *Look at the stars, Allie; look at the stars.*
> *I've never really noticed them before.*

The wedding was beautiful. We'd written our vows in the car on the way up, and Winston cried as he said his, and my voice cracked with feeling as I said mine. We held each other's hands and heard our officiant, another friend — there were so many friends, so many who loved us — talk about what she had seen us love about each other. About the ways in which Winston had supported me, yes, but we all knew that, and so she talked about what I brought to the relationship. The times I carried him. She saw that our marriage was an extension of a promise that had already been made, that day I'd sat up in bed and turned on the light and told him what was probably growing in the middle of my head, and he had decided to stay. And we ate, and danced, and at some point, standing by the cliff on which we got married, I saw an eagle or a hawk or some other kind of raptor swooping around. Allison had loved birds, written entire books of poetry dedicated to birds. And so I whispered to myself, *Allison, I see you. Allison, thank you for being here. Allison, thank you for everything. Allison, thank you for loving me.*

Our wedding was more than a marker that we were beginning our lives together; it was also a way for me to say goodbye to Allison. To accept that she wasn't there. To let myself try to begin to move on. To move through.

Still, her presence was everywhere, locked deep into my burned heart. I felt, during the wedding, as though I was finally able to let the love in. My friends from college, with whom I had reconnected in the course of my recovery, who had stayed a part of my life through changes in geography, sexual orientation, focus, illness, came. I knew that they were coming because they loved me. My friends from grad school, who had long ago stopped being my competition, came. My closest girlfriends did a coordinated dance with me in the center. One of them even picked me up and swung me around.

I was in the warm embrace of my family. I was in the warm embrace of my friends. I could feel the love and I trusted Winston to love me forever because Allison had taught me what it felt like to be loved unconditionally, and I knew that that was how he loved me.

I trusted that this was the end of the struggle. I didn't have brain cancer. I was in love. I was loved. That was all that mattered.

～

Five days later it fell apart.

act three

seven

~

O nce I started paying attention, I realized that I wasn't the only sick person my age. Shortly before I'd started dealing with a brain surgeon, I'd watched a college friend of mine decline in health, a process she documented on Facebook. The story was that she had gone to the doctor after having a 104-degree fever for ten days, was told it was conversion disorder, a.k.a. hysteria, and walked home. That was the last time she walked for longer than ten minutes. She posted on Facebook about her experiences with unrelenting fatigue, difficulty reading, difficulty walking. She described a burning spinal cord, brain inflammation. She posted pictures of herself with neurological sensors taped to her head, waiting to be pushed into a scanning tube. Of a newly acquired wheelchair.

I watched my friend post updates about experimental dietary restrictions — no gluten, no dairy, no vinegar, no soy sauce. I watched her search for an answer, and then find one: she was diagnosed with chronic fatigue syndrome, a terrible name for an even more terrible disease, and one with no standard treatment. I watched her try heavy-duty anti-biotics and heavier-duty antivirals. I watched her cross the continental United States in search of sympathetic doctors. I watched her begin to make meaning of her experience, and then I watched her say that she was going to make a movie about people experiencing the same thing that she had. Over the years that we were sick, a continent apart but in some ways tandem, I felt like she was winning the illness Olympics with her breadth of suffering, treatment, and also artistic production. I was just high-key uncomfortable, was constantly terrified, and couldn't figure out how to find any kind of creative value in my experience.

And there were other differences. By being diagnosed with a misunderstood disease, she was entering a world I'd never had to be in; my problems were visible on MRI films, in EKG prints. And so I wanted to believe her, and I *mostly* believed her, but at the same time, I found myself wondering. Why did she need to go to one specific doctor, and only that specific doctor? Why was she trying so many different things? Why couldn't she get better? I watched her solve mystery after mystery. I also watched her get tremendous relief from pursuing serious mold avoidance via living in a tent in her backyard. Every time I watched her find a new answer within the diagnostic umbrella of chronic fatigue syndrome, and try a new treatment, I felt—though guilt-ily—a rush of relief that at least I knew what was wrong with me. That my problems had taken a long time to diagnose, but that in the end they had recognizable symptoms and names: Rathke. Wolff. Parkinson. White.

～

And yet, as I saw her describe her symptoms, as I watched video clips she posted, as I learned more about what it was like to live in her body, it was getting harder and harder for me to quiet the tiny voice that told me, scratching at the back of my mind, that, with me, there was so much more that was wrong.

~

Before the beginning of all of my dramatically measurable medical events, I had also experienced less explicable symptoms: a waxing and waning dizziness, cognitive problems, sleeplessness and night sweats, loss of appetite and loss of energy. I was exhausted almost all the time, pale, with near-coal-black circles under my eyes. Sometimes I felt better and often I felt worse, for no discernible reason. Since first losing my appetite after moving in with Leila eight years before, I'd never really felt hungry. No one had ever really confirmed that my brain hemorrhage, or Wolff-Parkinson-White, or the ovarian cysts that had also shown up on ultrasounds were behind those symptoms, but we had all been so distracted by the imminently life-threatening issues that we'd put them to the side.

"It's *possible*," my doctors had said, again and again and again, when I'd asked if perhaps the bodily effort of growing maybe-tumors or dealing with extra heart pathways was making me so tired. "We don't really know."

Even though I knew something was still wrong, I took every chance I could get to edge myself farther from the world of the sick and closer to the world of the well. I pretended that these other symptoms were gone. I clamped down on the dizziness I felt whenever I walked into the school library, treated my constant and lingering nausea by chewing raw ginger every day. The story, after all, was that we had thought I would be very sick but I was not. I did not want the story to be that I had been very sick and then I had gotten better but actually I was still sort of sick, and maybe even sicker. My wedding had felt like my way of marking a turning point, a return to caring about things like new ideas, interesting work projects, what books to read. As much as being sick had shown me that I was loved, I was still so relieved to be out of the world of pain and doctors and uncertainty and fear that I tried to force my body to be finished.

But then: one week after our wedding I got dramatically sick again, seemingly with the flu, but this time I really couldn't get better.

"I haven't been regular sick in so long, I forgot how *miserable* it is!" I said to Winston. I *had* forgotten. I'd stopped commiserating with people about the indignities of the body. It's hard to find people to relate to about how hard it is to function with half your pituitary scraped off, about the emotional paralysis that comes with finding out you have a heart defect that could kill you any second. But the flu? As Allison used to say, "Oh god, THE FLU! Praise the flu!" I reveled in its normalcy.

But then it stopped being so normal. It sort of got better, but not all the way. *I* sort of got better, but not all the way. I was trying to get back to school, and so I was taking a writing workshop, and teaching a freshman writing seminar, and those should have been straightforward, but I started to lose my train of thought while I was teaching, or commenting on a colleague's short story. The freshman seminar was about architectural history, held twice a week at eight a.m., four stories underground in the oldest, most crumbling library on campus, and I found that I needed to gather within myself every molecule of energy I could to get myself to class. Once there, I had to corral focus into what felt like a sense of weightlessness in my brain. I remember many mornings, standing at the podium, coffee in hand, seeing eighteen sleepy and interested and bored faces staring back at me, with me having absolutely no idea what I'd just been talking about. My sentences were full of gaps. I talked around it, played around with it, never showing how frightening these gaps in my immediate short-term memory were.

I'd always loved the classroom, felt like I got it, loved the performance, the excitement, the reading of the room, the tiny but crucial energetic shifts that happen even in a lecture, the way in which I saw my students begin to grow, to unwind their own thoughts, to argue — over buildings! over texts! — but now, suddenly I was losing all of that fire. Sentences dropped halfway through; words that had been on the tip of my tongue fell into a chasm that I could sense, with an itch just outside my peripheral vision, was opening up in my mind. I'd never felt both this present and this aware of a split. After brain surgery, when I'd been too out of it to do anything but watch TV, I hadn't really *realized* how out of it I was. But here, I was awake; I was present for my experience, and all I could feel was that I was starting to drift away. And there was the matter of my throat closing up, the feeling that no matter how deeply I breathed, how calmly I inhaled through my nose, I couldn't get enough air. Also, I couldn't eat anymore, not really. And, of course, I was tired. So very, very, very tired all the time.

No matter how tired I was, I couldn't sleep. I tried everything. No screens two hours before bed, which gave me two hours to take baths, do face masks, read books and magazines. I drank valerian tea. I'd found an integrative doctor who specialized in solving mysteries, and I asked him what to do, and he said,

"Well, if you're really having trouble, we'll give you the big guns," which I thought might be Ambien, but no, it was an herbal supplement with melatonin and . . . valerian.

It didn't work. No screens didn't work. Baths definitely didn't work. And it was strange, because right before getting into bed I felt exhausted, like I couldn't even drag myself into the bedroom, but as soon as I lay down and closed my eyes, everything felt hallucinatory. I saw images and colors, felt my heart start to race. I shifted positions — lying first on my side, then my back, then my stomach, trying to find a way to lie so that the pounding of my heart wouldn't keep me awake. I lit candles. I bought a plant. I meditated for five minutes before bedtime, using an app I'd downloaded from the internet. I did restorative poses, lying on the ground with my feet up on the bed. I put one hand on my sternum and one hand on my belly. I breathed. I didn't sleep.

I struggled on until one morning I woke up from another distracted, distressed, visually intense almost-sleep, and as I pulled our window shades up I noticed that the window frames were mottled and speckled with black dots. I'd noticed the dots before, had spent an afternoon leaning out the window, spraying with Windex and wiping, paper towel after paper towel accumulating dark brownish-black grime. I had thought it was just dirt, layered on through years of dust and urban detritus, but now I thought it might be something else. I looked closer, and this time read the dots as the mold spores they were. I drafted an email to our landlord—*mold on window frames*—but didn't send it because I didn't want to be a bother, and I'd heard mold could be bad for people with asthma, but I didn't have asthma, so it was probably just a nuisance. The thought of my college friend's extreme mold avoidance popped into my head. I pushed it away. I saved the email in my drafts folder on my way out the door to see my mystery-solving doctor, hoping he could help figure out some of the vagueness that was wrong with me.

"Have you ever noticed any mold in your house?" he asked after hearing how every single symptom had gotten worse.

After earlier visits, he'd tested me for everything else he could think of—Lyme (negative), celiac (negative), parasites (positive but, apparently, nothing to worry about and totally normal!), anemia (extremely positive but easily treatable)—and we'd always come up blank for any kind of overarching explanation. We were into new territory here.

As soon as he said "mold," I startled.

"I literally *just* drafted an email to my landlord about it," I said.

"Case closed," he said. "You're really sensitive to mold."

"So being allergic to mold could be affecting *everything*?" I'd just listed every single functional system and told him how badly it was working.

"It's not really an *allergy*," he said. "It's a fundamental inability to process mycotoxins; I've seen some people get *really* sick." His daughter, he told me, was one of them. It had taken her two years to figure it out. He told me that she'd recovered by getting rid of everything, moving, and staying away from moldy places. In the split second before he said the next sentence, I convinced myself that his daughter must have been much sicker than I was. I wouldn't have to get rid of everything, move, and stay away from moldy places.

"So, the good news is there's a solution," he said. "The bad news is that you have to get rid of everything you own, move, and definitely stay away from moldy places."

Move? What did he mean? Apartments? Neighborhoods? Cities? *States?*

"I'd get out to Walnut Creek," he said. It was drier out there, but if Winston and I moved to that suburb it would mean adding a notorious commute to both of our lives. "And try and get a place with new construction—it'll be a lot less likely to be moldy."

Did he think I had infinite financial resources? Did he think I could just move, tomorrow? That I could go from paying under two thousand dollars a month for a serviceable (though moldy) apartment in the flats of Oakland to a luxury high-rise in one of the richest suburbs in the state?

"Is there a way to test for this? To make sure it's really this?"

He gave me a name for a mold inspection company he liked to use.

"They check the air, which is important."

And in the meantime, were there any other options?

"Can I just . . . get someone to clean?"

"No," he said. "Everything's contaminated—you can't get the spores out."

I trusted him, because a few months earlier he'd been the only person to think to test me for anemia, had found and corrected a crippling ferritin deficiency, and he was kind.

He was compassionate. I could sense, whenever I listed my problems, that instead of being annoyed or looking forward to when I was out of his office, he believed that something was wrong with me.

"You shouldn't be feeling this bad," he said to me over and over and over again, when he could sense that I was on the verge of giving up, that I was trying to just convince myself that it would be easier to stop trying.

I understood why my college friend had flown across the country to see one specific doctor; I understood now why bedside manner matters. When I wasn't in this doctor's office, I could feel myself always downplaying my symptoms. Surely everyone got tired. Surely everyone got dizzy if they went outside, or inside. Surely all of my fellow graduate students had my kind of insomnia; they all complained about some form of sleeplessness, anyway. I remembered a friend of mine, years earlier in New York, talking about the frustration she felt with her mother, who'd been sick and undiagnosed for years.

"One day it's her thyroid and then the next it's her blood sugar," my friend said. "I'm just like, 'Okay, move *on*.'"

No one had told me to move on, but I kept trying to tell myself to move on. I was caught in the interstice between believing that these waxing and waning symptoms were part of learned sickness behavior — that my body wasn't really suffering the way I could sense it was, that this was some post-traumatic stress response to the surgeries and the cancer fear — and the deep well of knowledge screaming to me that something was terribly wrong. So when my doctor said things like "I believe you," and "You should be falling asleep and staying asleep," and "No, something's wrong," of course

I was going to listen to his advice. I was much more interested in a physical diagnosis than an emotional one.

There was also a tiny flicker of . . . hope? Something I realized as soon as I felt it spark that I had assumed would always be absent.

Allison had always reminded me to have hope.

"If we don't have hope, we don't have anything," she said that day she brought her CT scan home, the one that showed her liver full of innumerable tumors. She said it again the day I hopelessly showed her the line of my tumor marker, rising, rising, rising. How could *she* have hope? What was it that she was hoping for? In retrospect, I realized: peace, serenity, a sense of having lived a good life. The experience of hope itself, the way it lights the heart. In the last years of her life, Allison lived in the infinite space inside hope. She did not think that she would be cured; she did not believe that she would get better. But she hoped for the sake of experiencing hope itself. That was enough for her. And that was what I felt in the office.

"This will help in the meantime," he said as he wrote the supplement name on a prescription pad. "But the real treatment is moving."

"Got it."

"And I'm serious: you *have* to get rid of everything porous."

"Porous?"

"Fabric, paper. Anything upholstered. Anything that isn't glass or steel, basically."

My thirty-minute consult was up.

"Anything else I should do?" I asked. I knew he was leaving for Tahiti, wanted to make sure I was all set until he got back.

"Just stay off the internet. Stay away from the mold people. Do *not* end up in a tent in Arizona."

The next time we spoke, it was from my tent in Arizona.

~

I came home from the doctor, walked in the door, and told Winston we had an answer, finally, to why I'd never recovered from the flu, to all those other symptoms that had plagued me.

We looked at the apartment again. There was mold everywhere. A line of black specks marched across our dining room table. We looked at the window in his closet—covered in mold. We walked into our kitchen, where Winston, meaning well, had installed safety guards on the windows so that they couldn't be opened all the way from outside, which meant we'd never really aerated the kitchen. I flashed back to moisture collecting on the windows every time I cooked. How hadn't I put this together? The cutting board wasn't dirty; it was moldy. The edges of the window frames were crusted with mold. I could see that everything that was wood had been warped, completely, with mold.

I gave away all of our books, had my friends take all my clothes to Goodwill, shredded every paper document I wasn't sure I wanted, and posted a hundred times on Facebook about getting rid of all my stuff.

In other words, I went into full-on mold panic.

After I had posted online that I was searching for a place

to live, options flooded my way. I spent hours driving around Berkeley, checking out apartment after apartment. I agreed to sublet rooms, rent apartments, and then changed my mind once I visited and—always, always—found mold: flecks on the windowsill, fuzz behind the fridge. I knew the Bay Area is a geographical bathtub—that famous fog? Moisture. Mold.

After a few weeks of looking, convinced that my apartment was completely unsafe for me, I called my in-laws; I'd been to their house and never felt sick. Winston's mother and I had bonded over occasional teas; I'd asked her permission to marry him after he'd asked Alex. I felt close to them, and I trusted them, and I also relied on their sense of spirituality to nudge them in the direction of helping me. They're deeply religious; if nothing else, I thought, they'd feel compelled to be kind.

"Of course you can come! We'll set up Win's old bedroom for you," they said when I asked if I could just stay with them for a few days and regroup.

I showed up that evening, hastily packed computer, phone, wallet—I needed to get all new clothes—in hand. They led me to his basement room, with a perfectly made-up bed. There was carpeting everywhere in their basement; it occurred to me that as much time as I'd spent in their house, I'd never spent any in their basement, although I'd noticed that every time I opened the door that went from the kitchen down, there was a peculiarly sharp smell.

I didn't sleep.

"You're not gonna believe this, but . . . I think the room is moldy," I said the next day, sitting at the breakfast table and trying to get some work done before the day's fatigue kicked in.

"You're okay in the main floor of the house, though, right?" his mother asked.

Yes, I was. They brought down a twin mattress, and my mother-in-law ordered a plastic mattress protector, and they moved their dining room table out of the way, and there I slept, in the corner of their dining room. Just for a few days (that turned into six weeks).

Ironically, it was when I was at this lowest, sickest point that my income skyrocketed. I was desperate—moving is never cheap, and neither is throwing out every single thing you own and starting over—so I did the only thing I could think to do: I began to ask for what my skills were actually worth. I wondered why it took my being so sick to finally ask for what I deserved—had probably been worth for years. It was that permission again, the one Allison had taught me about; how the desperation and isolation of illness can also lead to a freedom, a sense of expanded possibility. Sometimes that's falling in love. Sometimes it's taking a chance on a wild diagnostic possibility. Sometimes it's asking for a very high day rate. I worked out a deal with a friend to ghostwrite her memoir; it paid well, and monthly. An architecture firm that needed help with their communications began paying me a retainer to write all of their editorial copy and strategize publicity. Having the prospect of more money freed me up to do so much: look at newer apartments, buy supplements, not worry so much about having to completely replace all of my clothes.

At the same time, the complexity and insecurity of my situation was becoming increasingly harder to deal with. I felt like I was starting to have reactions to *everywhere,* even environments without visible mold: cars, restaurants, brand-new apartments. By the time I'd been staying with Winston's parents for two weeks, I'd signed and broken three leases. Every time I signed a lease, I thought the brand-new or barely used apartment in Walnut Creek, or Berkeley, was perfect, but every time I tried to move in, or clean, I started feeling that familiar symptom: the slow encroaching loss of focus, the feeling that my head was trying to depart my body, burning eyes, a flushed face.

Of course I began to doubt myself. I could see how this looked from the outside. I could feel the desperation in my Facebook posts, in how sunny and bright I tried to keep my attempts at finding a sunny and bright apartment. I could feel how hard I was trying to convince everyone else how real this was, because I could barely believe it myself. Was there really mold everywhere?

Some people thought so.

Over Facebook, through my college friend, I connected with a science writer and chronic fatigue syndrome patient named Julie Rehmeyer. She was public about how she'd essentially cured her chronic fatigue syndrome by avoiding mold, and she was a science writer with bylines in the *New York Times,* the *Washington Post, Discover.* She was legit. She'd won a fellowship for a year in Boulder to write a book about her experiences, which meant that her Santa Fe house, mold-proof and good for her, was available for rent. Moving to a stranger's house in the middle of the New Mexico landscape felt like the nuclear option, and my mold-aware doctor *had* warned me against moving into a tent in the desert, but this wasn't a tent, it was a house! And besides, I needed a nuclear option.

Winston knew how desperate I was. He knew that as much as I loved his parents, I couldn't sleep on their dining room floor forever. We all knew that as much as they loved me, at some point they'd enjoy having their dining room occupied just by a table instead of a freaked-out daughter-in-law. He also knew how hard I'd tried to find an apartment in our area. And so I told him about this option, laying out the pros.

"It'll just be a chance for me to reset," I said. "I think if I just get clear of mold for a year, maybe we can come back."

Julie had said her sensitivity had gone way down after a full year of intensive mold avoidance. Winston's internship was ending in August anyway, which was when the house would be available. That seemed like kismet. And also, Santa Fe was near Sandia National Laboratory, and maybe he could get a job there, or maybe he just wouldn't have a job for a year, which would be fine because I was making more money than we'd ever imagined either of us would make. I also acknowledged the cons. We didn't know anyone in Santa Fe. We'd just gotten married. And more important even than the two-person family we'd begun to construct, I felt like I was finally reaping the emotional rewards of my extravagant medical situation. Our wedding ceremony had explicitly involved our friends; we'd said "I do," but we'd also asked our friends to stand up and say "We do," when asked by our officiant if they would stand by us through sickness and health, would help us remember to come back to each other if we ever felt like forgetting.

After years and years of feeling like I couldn't connect,

or was on the periphery, I'd finally found my people. And even though Allison was dead, her presence was everywhere in Berkeley. I thought of her when I turned the corner on Ashby and Telegraph and saw the Whole Foods where once we'd gone together and later I'd gone for her. When I missed her so much that all I could do was silently scream, I could sit outside her house, drink a Diet Coke, and eat coffee ice cream in her honor. Her memory was more than something I had to keep alive; it infused the air. She occupied the streets of Berkeley and Oakland; I heard her voice, saw green Hondas and forgot for that second that she was dead. Leaving would mean not only leaving my community, but also the way in which the fact of Allison's life saturated every day of mine. Leaving would require accepting that she was gone, something I never thought I'd be ready to do.

Winston agreed because he could see how sick I felt every moment, how lost and confused I was. He could sense my desperation. I needed help, again. And he gave it to me.

eight

~

Julie and I arranged to Skype so that Winston and I could see the house and she and her husband, John, could meet us. Through our computer screens they gave us a tour of the house, a straw bale building she'd built herself. They were out in the open, on the land. It was safe. And it would be available in August.

I thanked all the gods that I had married someone who believed me. Who believed *in* me and my essential nature, which was (for the most part) rational, even-keeled, logical. After I'd signed and broken several leases, my mother called Winston directly, frantic with the thought that her daughter had become completely emotionally dysregulated, convinced that surely there must be something deeper going on, some sort of trauma-response problem. I worried, too.

~

I asked Winston every day if he thought I was making this up, if he thought I was overreacting.

"It's clear that *something's* going on that you're reacting to," he said.

I wanted him to full-on buy in. But he's forever a scientist: methodical, measured, willing to entertain a hypothesis but deeply invested in testing it. I make impulsive leaps, decisions based on hunches and feelings and hopes and fears. Winston starts at the beginning, works his way through. He believed that I'd been very sick after the flu. He remembered my slow and difficult recoveries from my surgeries. He believed that I'd been a little dizzy for years. He could see that there'd been mold in our closet and our window frames. Were they connected? He didn't have enough information to make a comprehensive scientific call. But he did believe me. He believed that I was having some sort of reaction. He held on to the person he had chosen to spend the rest of his life with, the person who had been (mostly) rational for the two years he'd known me. Yes, he told people who sidled up to him to ask what he thought about what was going on, of course he was worried, and of course he wondered, sometimes, if we were getting rid of all of our stuff because I was having a mental crisis rather than a physical one. But he had known and trusted me enough to marry me. He had vowed to be with me in sickness and in health, for better and for worse, and this was the worse, and we had often been in the worse, and he was with me.

"I remind myself that at her core, Eva is a rational and logical person," he told my mother, his brothers, his friends, anyone who was starting to murmur intimations of concern. I didn't feel rational and logical. I felt desperate, and tormented, and confused. And yet I believed in my body's signals, which were impossible to ignore.

I knew I had to trust myself. And still, I needed confirmation. So I went online, ignoring my doctor's warnings, and fell into a rabbit hole. Here I saw conspiracy theories, videos of experimental treatments going wrong, blog after blog about mold avoidance. Within this world, there were warring factions. One camp believed that mold caused chronic fatigue syndrome. Another believed that the mold theory couldn't be more wrong. A third believed that all unexplained illnesses were due to metabolic dysfunction. A fourth was sure that every disease could be traced to Lyme. A fifth the same, but this time with the Epstein-Barr virus. Every group had their preferred doctor, testing lab, treatment method. This was an entire medical community, full of naturopaths who insisted on testing strands of hair for mineral residues that would prove some problem on the mitochondrial axis that led to a C-reactive protein increase.

I entertained thoughts of joining one or more or all camps. Who was this doctor in Maryland who believed that "sick building syndrome" was the cause of all modern ills? How hard was it to get an appointment? I found an internet community called Mold Avoiders, who emphasized the kind of extreme mold avoidance that had seemed to cure Julie. Suddenly everything I'd ever believed in seemed like *it* was part of the conspiracy theory. According to the internet, it was mainstream medicine that was full of quacks and snake oil. Commenter after commenter on online message boards devoted to undiagnosed problems complained about their idiotic mainstream doctors who didn't even know how to read a B vitamin level. The first few days I spent online, I thought it was ridiculous. But then, slowly, it crept up on me: Wait a second—did *my* doctor know how to read a B vitamin level?

I felt as reliant on these strangers to give me information as I felt on Winston and my friends to keep reminding me that I wasn't in some protracted post-marriage fugue. But it was all so confusing, and all so inconsistent. Fish oil was either the greatest thing or the worst; you *had* to do a nebulizer silver spray if you had any hope of getting better. Obviously airway remodeling happened on a cellular level once you'd been exposed to a water-damaged building, and the only way out was through a nine-step process that included a veterinary drug in one of the tiers. Clearly autism was caused by a rise in gluten intolerance. Psychiatric problems were all traceable to mold! I felt myself inching further and further down.

I talked to Winston about some of what I found, but I kept ninety-five percent of it to myself. I hadn't promised him not to keep any secrets, I thought, when I heard myself translate a flurry of online activity into a simple "We need to move to Santa Fe." And he agreed. We decided that I'd leave as soon as possible, and he'd join me in August, when his job finished.

Despite all of my doubts, and whatever doubts they might privately have held, my friends reacted with sympathy and support to what they saw happening.

"I'll just have to come visit you a lot," one friend said when I told her I needed to move to Santa Fe.

"New Mexico's a little far for me, but I'll meet you in Arizona," another friend said.

"I think you'll love the desert!" said another.

As embarrassed as I felt about not knowing what was going on, as much judgment as I turned toward myself, that's how much empathy and compassion my friends showed me. To me, this was an existential crisis: Was I losing my grip on reality? Or was I sick?

I thought back to my skepticism about my college friend. My skepticism about the traumas of so many people, which hadn't made sense to me. I realized that I'd always relied on my own sense of what was right and true and necessary and important, that instead of reacting with compassion to someone else's method of dealing, I'd often reacted with judgment, with trying to figure out how I was safe in comparison. That's what judgment is all about, in the end. Safety. Allison had often talked to me about people's responses to her cancer—asking if she'd smoked (she had), or if she'd grown up under power lines (she couldn't recall), or if she was really doing the right treatment (how could we ever know?). We'd talked about the drive behind those questions. It wasn't really to figure out what was going on with her. It was often a mode of distancing, of assessing the differences. We translated this into: *You smoke, I don't. You have cancer, I won't.*

Once again, it was the love of others that showed me the way.

"What I see is how desperate you are to feel better," one friend said.

"I don't know what's going on, but I can see you're suffering," said another.

This was friendship without judgment. This was the kind of support I realized I'd never fully given anyone else;

I'd always been too scared to. I thought about other contexts, other times I hadn't believed women. A friend had said to me once that whatever we most judge is what we will eventually encounter. I had always judged abstractly sick people. I'd thought that they were probably exaggerating, or didn't know how to be tough with pain, or were just bored and looking for something to do. But I didn't come to that on my own; I wasn't alone in my sense of disbelief.

There have been countless essays, books, articles, podcasts, and now movies about hard-to-diagnose illnesses. A central theme is this: Women's pain is ignored. Women's pain is misunderstood. Women's pain is undertreated. There are horror stories about women turned away from the ER, diagnosed with "a touch of gas" when they were actually experiencing ovarian torsion, an excruciatingly painful condition in which the ovary twists, wrapping around itself, until it bursts. I've read newspaper articles about women in their midforties who died of ovarian cancer because doctors treated the early signs and symptoms—thickening around the middle, fatigue, night sweats—as hallmarks of womanhood, magazine stories about unrecognized thyroid problems that were diagnosed as stress. When I first got dizzy, I was diagnosed and rediagnosed with anxiety, and treated with psychotropic medication that, in retrospect, I never needed.

Until I got sick with what I believed was mold, though, I'd had my brain MRI results in my back pocket. When a doctor hypothesized that I was stressed, I was able to point to my brain surgery.

"Do you want to be the doctor who misses my next brain hemorrhage?"

"Fair. I'll order the tests."

But with this, I'd lost that trump card. I had no idea what was going on. My doctors had no idea what was going on. I was slipping into the nebulous world of "undiagnosed women," an ever-growing bucket into which women with conditions like Lyme, post-Lyme, Hashimoto's thyroiditis, unusual presentations of diabetes, and on and on, often fall.

At the same time that I desperately wanted a credible diagnosis, I also kind of wanted someone to intervene. There was part of me that still hoped I was just having a stress reaction, that if someone bullied me out of it I would get better. Stop malingering. My mother's skeptical call to Winston was the singular voice for that side, but once we Skyped and she saw how out of it and exhausted I was, even she came around.

"There's definitely something wrong with you, kiddo," she said. "You're *really* out of it."

And there were some who were more laconic. Who said things like "I hope you find a solution soon," and "All we want is for you to feel better." I wanted them to say things like "We believe you," and "Mold! Who knew?!" But why did I expect that when I hadn't granted it to others?

It reminded me of all the subtle ways in which I'd been taught not to believe women. And it wasn't limited to illness. I thought about reports of sexual violence or assaults, devastating stories I'd heard from friends but that I'd decided were too distressing for my worldview to believe. It sounds awful, but it was easier for me to believe that the world was fundamentally safe and they were fundamentally misunderstanding something than it was for me to see how prevalent violence was. How prevalent, in my case, illness was. During my first hospitalization, I'd had a doctor say that they might never figure this out. That medicine wasn't as reliable as it was on *Grey's Anatomy*. I didn't believe her then. I still wanted not to believe her. How could there be infinite mysteries within the human body? How could there not be a way of just figuring something out?

I didn't want to be learning this lesson about trust: of self, of others. But here I was, once again being shown the way by my friends.

Allison was still helping me, even after death. I remembered that she had taught me how to slow down, to elbow out room for laughter and joy in the in-between of not knowing. Everyone else had taught me about the inexhaustible love that is present in deep friendship. Before, I'd had a next scan or next surgery to point to. Here, I had only some abstract hope: Santa Fe, a mold-free house. But having the next touchstone reminded me of something Allison had said to me once, that life is a process of swimming to the next buoy, even when we feel like we have a sea to cross.

"We don't swim across the ocean all at once," she'd said. "We just swim to the next buoy — with help."

She had taught me that it was okay that I couldn't fix her cancer, or take her pain away. She had taught me that just my being next to her was enough. For the last year of her life, I'd been swimming next to her, sometimes reaching the buoy first to keep it stable for her, sometimes trying to catch up while she held it down. I didn't have Allison anymore, though I had her voice, brushing the back of my mind with every breath. But I had everyone at home, and someone who could swim next to me, could point to the next buoy. Someone who I knew believed me. Someone who told me that, every single day.

I had my friend Lauren.

~

A few months earlier, Lauren and I had planned that she would come visit me in the Bay Area as soon as I found a new home. We'd met in an online group for women who were sober and liked to use all caps on the internet, two salient and overlapping interests, and she'd called me one day from a wedding, asking for advice on how to get through the reception without drinking, and once we'd had voice contact we established a more regular text and email thing, and then, a few months before getting married, I flew to Seattle for a writing assignment, and we met and loved each other immediately, and so we were friends. She is a freelance writer and can therefore work from anywhere, and so a few months before the wedding she flew down and stayed on my couch for four days, bringing matching pajamas, and we lay on my couch in pink pajamas printed with pictures of milk and cookies and the term BFF: best friends forever. She came to my wedding too, and gave a tremendous speech about why Winston and I had walked down the aisle to a *Doctor Who* song, and she and I slow-danced together to another *Doctor Who* song.

Lauren was sympathetic that I had been sick, but my body wasn't the focus of our friendship. She had her own experience with the abyss of chronic illness, with the daily grief that comes from internal revolt, from the fervent wish that the contours of a life be different. A psychic told her once that she lives at two extremes, flipping between two poles. She has bipolar disorder. When we were together, we talked about other things besides our conditions: how bad I am at thinking critically about television, how much we both love reality dating shows, candy (I love sour candy, she loves Snickers), the joys and sorrows of Twitter. We were able to be emotional together, mostly because of Lauren's incredible range, the level to which she's always front and center with her feelings. Where she wants to be a sea sprite, I want to be a robot. I am a block of concrete where she is a beanbag chair.

"I just made another lifelong friend," she'll say after spending three minutes in line to get coffee. I would rather get another brain surgery than have to make small talk with strangers.

And yet inside, we are so similar. What she expresses, I feel. I might have *wanted* to cry at how connected to her I felt so early on in our friendship, but Lauren was the person who actually cried. During Winston's and my wedding ceremony, I remember looking out into the audience and zeroing in on her face, on the tears running down her cheeks. I felt as happy and awed and overwhelmed by love as she did, but I wasn't able to show it the way she was. She opened up a path for deeper emotional intimacy.

So, she'd planned to come. But after I kept postponing her visit, and then admitted that I didn't have a place for her to stay because I didn't have a place for myself to live, I asked her if she felt up for something a little different: a desert road trip, maybe to Sedona, which I knew was dry and which Jason had recommended for a drying-out break.

I played it up as a fun hang, just two girls chilling in the desert, getting spa massages and going for hikes, me running out the clock until Julie's Santa Fe house would be available. What I actually needed was someone to take care of me, and it couldn't be Winston, who was finishing an internship he couldn't in good conscience abruptly leave. I was terrified to be alone. Even back in Oakland, it had been a challenge to trust my body to even drive to Walnut Creek. I knew I needed to get to the desert. I also knew enough to know that I needed a friend.

nine

~

Lauren and I agreed to meet in Flagstaff. Scared of what
might happen to my body if I flew, I decided to drive.

The seeming endlessness of the western landscape felt
like a geographical marvel. I hadn't spent much time in the
middle of the continent; apart from a few years in Edmonton, I'd only ever lived near the coasts. Eugene was an hour
or so from the Oregon coast, and though I hadn't visited the
ocean that frequently, I'd always felt a deep sense of acces-
sibility, of connectedness to the rest of the world, via my rel-
ative proximity to the sea. Flying over Salt Lake City one
day when I was twenty-two, I'd marveled at how the city
just grew from nowhere, how the edges turn into the center. But Edmonton, where I'd spent my early adolescence,
wasn't that different; it was just that I understood how its
maps worked, where in relation to the world it lay. I realized
that some places seemed to be rootless, groundless, but they
weren't, not once you knew them.

I made my way through tiny towns, stopping for the
night in Parker, Arizona, then driving straight for hours.

Late afternoon the day after I'd left Oakland, I arrived at the Flagstaff airport. I pulled up to the curb and saw Lauren standing there, holding a single carry-on. She was wearing a sundress. She hugged me, held me tight.

"Oh, buddy," she said.

"I'm so glad to see you," I said. She hugged me again.

We took the 89A, winding through first forest and then past the red rocks, the famous red rocks that I realized I'd seen pictures of in coffee table books. We swung around and around hairpin curves, descending thousands of feet in thirty minutes, going from the cool mountain air of Flagstaff to the burning heat of Sedona.

We drove through the touristy part, past pizza restaurants with outdoor tables and water misters. We saw crystal store after crystal store, signs advertising psychics, energy healing, laser allergy elimination treatments. What was this place? Vibes were everywhere.

We found the hotel, checked in.

"Business or pleasure?"

I wasn't sure. I was still trying to make this be a fun vacation. I was also trying to save my own life.

". . . TBD?" I said. But no matter: the room seemed clean, and dry, and good.

"I think you'll be okay here," Lauren said, feeling the air and sensing my mood. She was already taking over.

We got dinner at the Whole Foods. A salad with roast chicken and without any dressing for me. Mac and cheese for Lauren. I'd found a list of foods that were supposed to be moldy, and I was avoiding all of them. No vinegar, no soy sauce, no gluten, no dairy, no corn, no sugar. Since I had stopped drinking I had used food to soothe myself when stressed—now I couldn't do that. No more cupcakes or pizza or sour candy or gummy worms or macaroni and cheese, no more *I don't drink so I deserve it.* I had to make do with meat and vegetables, with drinks made of spinach and green tea extract and lemon. Easy ways I used to eat didn't work anymore. I couldn't just eat a block of cheese when I thought I needed protein. I bought hard-boiled eggs, and started actually paying attention to the raw cashew desserts in the cold case.

The next day I felt better, and then the day after that I felt worse. There was a moment when I felt perfect, and I called Winston.

"I know it's so weird that I'm here, but I have to tell you, I feel better than I have in literally *years*," I said.

I was standing on the roof deck, the sun beating on me. Up above me was a majestic red rock. I could see its striations, the little shrubs of green sprouting out. I'd never seen this much rock, had never cared this much about rocks. I found it beyond beautiful. It was compelling.

"That's all that matters," he said.

It seemed like evidence. No matter what diagnostic slot I might or might not fit into, no matter what else was going on, I could *feel* that I felt better here. Being away from the Bay Area was working. All I had to do was stay on this path. Look ahead, never back to what I'd lost.

For the next three weeks, Lauren took care of me, mostly without my noticing. She'd bought a one-way ticket; we'd agreed to see how it went before she booked the return. I was grateful that she could work from anywhere, that her career as a TV critic required only internet access and a working laptop. She said she was hungry and we went and got food.

She told me she really felt like drinking Gatorade, so I did too. She reminded me that I liked doing yoga by making fun of herself for fake believing that there were only six poses, so I did some yoga in the room, just a few poses, the few I could remember. She never had to say that she believed my reactions, because she just acted like my mold sensitivity was a fact, washing her clothes in vinegar, which I'd heard was a good way to kill mold, laying them out in the sun to dry. She lived in rainy Seattle; we were sure her stuff was moldy. She'd brought a washable backpack instead of her preferred purse, stuffed her jeans in the freezer for twenty-four hours before coming, in an attempt to kill any spores. On other visits, she'd seen me eat gluten, ice cream, corn, all the things I suddenly said I couldn't eat anymore, and so she found me dairy-free coconut ice cream and energy bars packed with seeds and sweetened with agave. We ate nuts. She drank sodas and got cheeseburgers at McDonald's while I poured olive oil onto my plain salad. She made fun of me for the way I threw my clothes around the room, how I seemed incapable of keeping any sort of order in my physical environments.

"You are a feral *bear,*" she said one night as I pushed magazines and bags of coconut crisps and containers of cut-up watermelon, the closest I could get to sweets, to the side of my bed, making myself a tiny area in which I could curl up and try to fall asleep, the crackle of wrappers mixing with the thud of my phone—which I kept losing in the blankets— falling to the floor.

Her clothes were hung up in the hotel room closet, her various chargers carefully wound and put away in their own Ziploc bag. My jeans were thrown across the ottoman, my wet bathing suit creating a huge damp spot on the armchair, my phone charger crammed in my jacket pocket. In the mornings, when I worked on my friend's memoir or on the consulting work I was doing, she side-eyed me typing, hunched over my computer, a finger to my lips.

"You know I can't talk until ten," I said to her.

"Oh, right, your *savant* time," she said. She was referring to how fast I typed, to how intently I focused on my work in the mornings. But it wasn't because I was a brilliant savant. It was because even though there were moments where I felt amazing, every morning I was still racing against the onset of symptoms, just as I had in Berkeley. Not because I knew they'd come, but because I didn't know they wouldn't. Every day was a mystery: Could I make a plan for tomorrow? I never dared to.

Every night, we watched *The Real Housewives of Beverly Hills,* a show Lauren suggested for its complete nonrelevance to anything in our lives. She knew, intuitively, that anything more realistic would remind me of the life I'd left. *Real Housewives* reminded me that so much of what we were doing could — if I pretended hard enough — be categorized as some kind of out-of-context fantasy. We were just on vacation. We were just hardcore relaxing. There was nothing that was relatable, and so I didn't have to worry about my life being so far from what I'd remembered it being just two months earlier. We propped my laptop on an ice bucket that we propped on the ottoman that we had slid between our matching queen beds. By day she sat by the pool and I stayed inside, as cool as possible. By night she went swimming and I dipped my feet and then my legs in the pool, too scared of water from a childhood near-drowning incident to go in after dark. We went to sleep at nine and woke with the sun at six. Some mornings I was too weak to get up and so she went to get coffee.

"You get to be the king today," she said, walking out the door on her way to Java Love. We both knew it wasn't that I was the king. It's that she was offering a different narrative, even if just for a few minutes. It wasn't that I was too sick to walk across the street, she was saying. It was that I was too . . . fancy.

~

"Since you have a couple of weeks before you move in, do you want to come to Santa Fe and make sure the house works for you?" Julie wrote.

I hated researching anything before I leapt because it meant I might have to change my mind, usually publicly, due to my seemingly incorrigible practice of announcing things before they'd been finalized. I'd moved to New York without visiting, to Berkeley without visiting. I liked to leap, trust the net would appear, and then, often years later, I would come to understand what my motivations had really been.

"Do you think we should do it?" I asked Lauren.

"I guess as long as there's a Dairy Queen in Albuquerque I'll be fine," she said. I laughed.

Lauren told me later, much later, that she had been tracking me much more closely than I'd known. That when I picked her up, she wasn't sure I'd make it to the hotel. That I was paler than she'd ever seen me. That I seemed unfocused. That my eyes were glazed. That I didn't make all that much sense. It was alarming to hear how sick I'd been. Lauren had been on high alert the entire time. The jokes she'd made were signs of how much fun we were having; they were also diagnostic.

"I decided that if I could still get you to laugh, you were okay," she told me later, when we were marveling at what we had done together. But at the time, all I knew was that I was laughing. That she was keeping me safe. That as long as Lauren was there, I didn't have to be scared.

We made our way to Santa Fe, driving past the Santa Fe Opera House toward Julie's house, which was on a reservation about twenty-five minutes north of the city. I'd always pictured Santa Fe as an open desert town, bright and sunny. But the landscape was different from what I'd imagined; huge and ominous mesas lined the skyline in the distance. Everything felt brown. The rocks and the sky felt oppressive; there were clouds and gray and rain. I'd never felt so far from an ocean; I hadn't actually ever been so far from one. Even living in Edmonton, I'd been closer to the ocean than I was here.

This was land, true land, *the* land. The land of novels and movies and road trips and deep solitude. We turned off the main highway and onto a smaller road. We passed a store. Winston loved to walk to the store in the middle of the night for energy drinks, cigarettes. It was part of how he relaxed. How far would he have to walk, here? The road kept going, winding past a Four Seasons resort. How did so many people know about this part of the world to support a Four Seasons? How expensive was it? I looked, later. It was expensive. I knew from being a design writer that the fashion designer Tom Ford had built a $70 million Tadao Ando–designed ranch near here, the only Ando-designed residence in the entire country. That Julia Roberts had a ranch in Taos. New Mexico seemed to be full of some kind of magic that I just wasn't able to absorb. We kept driving.

"I don't know about this for Winston," Lauren said. I agreed, but I tried to shut the thought down. He would be miserable here, but I didn't know what choice I had. Or I did, but I couldn't fathom one. I'd decided to move to Santa Fe to get away from mold. That's what we had to do. We kept driving, and then the pavement stopped and we were on a dirt road. And then we were at the end of the dirt road — we were there.

The house looked smaller than it had online. Inside was open and airy, though. Julie shook my hand, and Lauren's.

"How are you feeling? Do you want to take a shower?" she asked.

I did, and said so, and showered, and after I'd washed the road and dust off, I asked Julie if I could use their landline for a consulting call with my architects since there wasn't any cell service out here. She agreed, and I went upstairs, took the cordless, and parked myself on the carpet. I called my clients, and did my best to be professional. I could feel that weight starting up again, could feel the way in which my brain was starting to go sideways, but I forced myself to be able to talk. Because I could remember what it felt like to be professional and talk about publication opportunities, I was able to slip into that mode. I could basically copy myself being a person; it was improvisational conversations that I had such a hard time with. We talked for thirty-five minutes and at the end of those thirty-five minutes I knew that there was something up here that I was reacting to. I felt a buzzing in my ears, a pressure throughout my sinuses. I was dizzy when I stood up. My stomach ached, my heart felt like it was being pinched, then stabbed. But it didn't make sense. How could Julie live here? How did she not notice how this felt? Frantic, I tried to calm my mind with information, just as I had when I'd looked at my tumor marker graph what felt like a lifetime ago. She had said that John's office was the "contamination room," where they put stuff they weren't sure about, or stuff that they were sure had mold. I'd been next to the room, but not in it. Could the toxins have escaped? Could they have settled? Had my airways been re-modeled? Did I need to do a silver nebulizer?

I went downstairs and found Julie. I started crying.

"I was upstairs, and I'm reacting to *something,*" I said. "I don't think this is going to work."

She was sympathetic, had been as desperate as I was. She recognized both the physical symptoms and the emotional exhaustion. But she's more can-do than I am. As I sobbed, she brusquely handed me a glass of water.

"Wasn't it this hard for you?" I asked. "Do you remember what this part was like?" I knew she'd had her own desert adventures.

"Sure, it was hard, but I just didn't really see the point in crying about it," she said.

I tried to pull myself together, but it was almost impossible. Trying to understand how this could be happening, that I was so sensitive to mold that a mold avoider's house was making me desperately ill, I missed the days of having a disease that made sense. I wished, just for a few brief and terrible seconds, that I could have just a bad brain MRI and concerning thickening on the pituitary stalk. I wished that I was just recovering from brain surgery, safe at home.

I wished for the simplicity of Wolff-Parkinson-White, a disorder that had a name and a standard treatment. I wished for the straightforwardness of excruciating pain.

It was six, and starting to get dark. I looked at Lauren, who was sitting at the picnic table. I could read her expression.

"I just don't know what to do, but I think we need to go," I said to Julie. I felt like crumpling. I felt bad about crying now that I'd seen how seemingly blasé she'd been. I felt like I wasn't doing a good job being a freaked-out newly diagnosed mold patient. I thought of what Allison had told me when I'd come to her after heart surgery. That I was doing a good job. That crying was the bravest thing to do. I thought about Allison. About what she would have made of this. She lived by Western medicine; chemotherapy kept her alive.

"I don't know about all that other stuff," she'd said, often, when a well-meaning person had suggested she try a celery juice diet. "I'm alive because of DRUGS."

I wanted to be alive because of drugs. I wanted to take all the medicines in the world, so long as they were available in pharmacies that were just regular pharmacies. My head was spinning with stories of detox supplements and mycotoxin-free coffee. I was listening to podcasts about drinking butter in the morning and how to make sure your mattress remained mold-free. I believed that it would have been so much easier to just be diagnosed with an awful thing and then die, but at least everyone would believe you that you just had the awful thing. And then I couldn't believe I'd thought that out loud, because Allison, who I loved more than anything, had been diagnosed with an awful thing and then she *had* died. Would she rather have had whatever was going on with me?

"Yeah, I don't think you can stay here," Julie said. We knew she meant this weekend, and this year. "I'll figure out what I want you to pay me." I was losing a safe haven. She was losing a tenant.

We got in the car, turned right onto the dirt road, headed for Albuquerque's clutch of airport hotels, which Julie said she'd heard online tended to be good. This was the kind of recommendation I was suddenly looking for: a hotel *with decent air.* We stopped for gas. Before I could even get out of the car, I turned to Lauren. I saw her face. I started crying. I couldn't stop. There was no air, suddenly. I opened my mouth to breathe but I couldn't catch my breath. I needed to scream, but I couldn't.

"I can't do this anymore, I don't understand what's happening to me, I don't know what the fuck is going *on,*" I managed to get out.

"Yeah, that was straight up the *worst,*" she said. "But you need to drive. We will *definitely* talk about this later, but it needs to be later, because I can't drive, and we need to get to a hotel, because you need to get in bed, and we need to stay there for *at least* two days."

She opened a bag of gluten-free, dairy-free, sugar-free, everything-good-free cacao seed energy lumps we'd bought earlier for $12.95 at Whole Foods.

"Eat this," she said.

"I can't," I said.

"I'm just going to sit here with this lump in my hand until you eat it," she said. I looked at her. I felt enough myself to roll my eyes.

"Do you see the face I'm making right now?" she said. It was a face she still makes, when she's pretending to be annoyed with me. A raised eyebrow and a pursed mouth. I laughed. I was still here. She could still get me back. I put a cacao seed lump in my mouth, chewed, swallowed. She handed me another two.

"Eat both of these," she said. "I know you can."

Lauren could sense what I was feeling. The despair of it. It wasn't just the loss of this particular option, or that I'd gotten, I believed, mold toxin–ed. She understood the magnitude of the loss that I was facing. I had been looking forward to this year in Santa Fe, this year of clean air and maybe writing a book or finishing my dissertation, of spending time with Winston, of having an adventure, and I had also believed that this would be my cure, my salvation, that all I needed was just some time in a pristine environment and I would be good, and now that was *gone*. And what did it mean that an environment a mold-sensitive person had thought was good was bad for me? Was I doubly sensitive? Triply sick? Did this mean I was so toxic that I couldn't tolerate even the slightest spore? Was something else wrong?

I finished the last cacao lump. I took a deep breath, and then another one. In and out through my nose. I used every single skill I'd ever developed in shutting myself down emotionally. Finally my skills at compartmentalization were useful. I put my hands on the steering wheel, by now such a familiar position. I put my foot on the gas. We drove. We drove past Santa Fe.

"Fuck you, Santa Fe," she said as we left the city limits and drove past the low adobe buildings that made up the suburbs. I gave Santa Fe the finger.

"Fuck you so hard, you fucking adobe-fucking-covered fucking piece of shit," I said. She laughed.

"Tell Santa Fe how you *really* feel," she said.

~

We drove all the way to Albuquerque, checked into a Court-yard Marriott. The room was good, clean, quiet. We went to the Applebee's across the parking lot for dinner. I ordered a salad with a burger patty on top, no dressing, no cheese, no onion on the burger. I was horrified at my restrictive-ness. For a brief period in my twenties I'd been a food writer, had prided myself on having no restrictions. I had always made fun of people with allergies and sensitivities. I thought they were just picky eaters hiding behind medical restric-tions, people who were scared to eat a little headcheese, or sea urchin. And then here I was, asking the waiter to take the tomatoes out of the salad, to give me the burger just plain on top. No butter anywhere, please. Cook only with olive oil, please. No corn on anything please. Just some tap water, please, thank you. I couldn't drink lemonade, or ginger ale. Just water, or some unsweetened iced tea.

We sat in silence. We hadn't been silent together since I'd picked her up in Flagstaff. The food came, and we ate in si-lence. I realized, as I started coming back into my body, back into myself, that Lauren had seen me, in the car, act in a way that no one had seen me: hysterical, truly desperate. I was in the booth of an airport-adjacent Applebee's, and to any-one else I looked pretty fine, and I'd never felt more afraid. Looking at Lauren, I felt like all of my insides were suddenly on the outside. I didn't know what to do. Worse, I was with another person who *knew* that I didn't know what to do. I had always at least believed that I knew what to do. Always. And here, I didn't even know what to say.

I'd always felt like silence meant that I was doing something wrong. I'd felt the compulsion to fill it, something I read later women did more than men, and so I'd tried to train myself to sit in the silence, not to jump in first. But the silence had always felt tense; like my interlocutor and I were both waiting for the other person to speak. Here, with Lauren, the silence felt like something else: a deep pool of everything that didn't need to be said. An infinite expanse of understanding. I had been so busy solving my problem since the day my doctor had told me to get away from mold that I felt like this was the first break I had given my brain. I'd avoided silence or rest because I hadn't felt capable of absorbing the decisions that I had to make. If I kept talking about leaving my entire life, and Allison's ghost, to move to the desert, I wouldn't have to accept that I was leaving my entire life, and Allison's ghost, to move to the desert. Silence, when I was frantically trying to get better, had been the enemy. Silence would have allowed room for doubt, and I did not believe that I could entertain even the slightest detour. But something about Lauren's face, the way she seemed perfectly self-contained, the way she smiled at the waiter when he walked by, the way she looked pointedly at my burger and pointedly back to me, the way in which we were able to communicate with brief moments of eye contact but mostly just the enveloping symphony of forks and chewing and sips of water that we were creating, was the salve my mind and body needed.

As I let myself fall into the comfort she was weaving around me, I realized that I needed Lauren's help to figure out what to do next. And that's when I realized that there was still another layer of friendship that I had yet to experience. Even when I'd felt so close to my friends, and to Allison, I'd still been in charge. I'd believed that only I truly knew what needed to happen. I had called the shots, handed out information and decisions like gifts, tiny markers of intimacy that I gave to those I felt safe with. As much as I'd asked Allison for her counsel, I'd never really believed that I didn't know my next right step, that I'd actually change my mind. But with Lauren, I wasn't in control of the information. I didn't have a plan. I didn't even know how to make a plan. I was unfocused. I was sure I was anemic again. My brain didn't work. I was weak and exhausted and hadn't eaten a carbohydrate in three weeks. I didn't know what to do. Stay at the Albuquerque Sunport hotel forever? I'd read online about people who did that, who just moved into safe hotels and did their best. Was I there? Wasn't I still better? I could still bounce back. But what to do?

Lauren suggested we go back to Sedona, just to regroup. I agreed.

And then, a few days later, eighteen days after she first flew to Flagstaff, Lauren turned to me while we were sitting at the pool.

"I love you so much, and I have to go home," she said. "I don't think my brain can do this anymore."

The inconsistency of our travels was starting to wear on her own brain chemistry; if she didn't leave, we'd both be in trouble. I interrupted her before she could even say the next prepared sentence.

"Oh my god, of course, of course," I said.

Acknowledging that she'd spent eighteen straight days next to me during what was then the most difficult period of my life felt almost impossible, and so instead of thanking her, or talking about my gratitude, I just tried to give her permission to leave.

"I'm doing so much better, dude. I'll be okay," I said. But inside: *Would I?*

"I think I've taught you everything you need to know to stay alive," she said. "You need to eat, and sleep, and rest, and stay out of the sun, and wear sunscreen."

I nodded.

"And drink Gatorade, bro." I nodded.

I was trying not to cry. Had I really absorbed all the lessons Lauren had taught me? About resting, and not pushing myself, and believing myself even when it felt like I was starting to slip into some kind of alternate reality? What was I going to do without her?

As much as I was deeply attuned to Winston, and the rest of my friends, it was with a different sort of care, and always a level of independence, both performed and real. With Lauren, I could fall into not knowing what to do. That day in the Applebee's, when I hadn't known what to do, had shifted the way in which I trusted her, in which I was able to trust another person.

ten

~

For the next three weeks I didn't speak to another human unless I was checking into a motel or buying food. I made a vague plan to drive in a square, following the plateau back through Albuquerque, up through Boulder, west to Utah, then back down to Arizona, in search of a place where mold and the environment wouldn't bother me so much, and, just as important, where Winston could find work. Sedona was great for me, but I didn't see a lot of opportunities for physicists. Boulder, Denver, Salt Lake City—those were dry cities, and also actual urban metropolises. Later, I would realize that I didn't need to sacrifice my health for him. That my need to live somewhere dry maybe felt extravagant, but wasn't. But I still felt guilt, and shame, that I was dragging my very new husband away from his home. I wanted to act like part of a couple, make decisions for both of us, even if I hadn't seen him in weeks, even if this illness felt like it was isolating me even from my most beloved. I drove from Sedona to Albuquerque in one day and checked into the Courtyard Marriott to rest for three nights, because that's what Lauren had told me to do. The next morning, I left for Colorado.

Every so often, I pulled over and pulled up my Maps app, when I had service, and looked at the blue dot that was supposed to locate me. I felt an encroaching panic, an agoraphobia I hadn't felt since I'd been eleven, walking across a school field and terrified of its open blankness. Once again, I used every mental trick I knew to shut myself down, to store my fear for later. One day I would be safe again. I promised that to myself. I touched the car, the steering wheel, the dashboard. I talked to myself, out loud, the sound of my voice feeling so foreign.

"You're doing the right thing, you're doing the right thing, you're doing so good," I said to myself, over and over and over again.

When the terror and the wide-open space felt too overwhelming, I pulled over by the side of the road and called Lauren, sobbing.

"I can't do this, I can't do this, I don't know what I'm doing."

"Oh, pal," she said. "It's so hard. Have you eaten?"

Her voice asking me if I'd eaten reminded me of Allison, who'd always asked me if I'd eaten. After I'd gone on and on about something for half an hour, she would say, gently,

"Oh, babe, that sounds so hard, and have you eaten?"

I never had. Lauren's care was so reminiscent of Allison's, but it was also her own. She knew what I was dealing with; she'd seen it up close. I kept reminding myself that she believed me. Sometimes I had to ask her to say so.

"I believe you, buddy," she said. Her voice on the phone, coming through the Mazda itself, became a lifeline.

"Oh hiiiii," she said when our voices connected. "How you doing, buddy?" I didn't have to explain.

"Ugh."

"I know. Have you eaten?"

∾

As I drove, I held on to Lauren's belief in me, to Winston's. To my friends, who texted to check in, who told me, implicitly and explicitly, that they trusted me. And yet they weren't with me all the time. They weren't with me during those hours of straight, flat highway, during the other hours of rolling mountain. They weren't with me when I stopped to order lunch, when I watched tourists who were so happy to be here, who were loving the freedom of their road trips. They couldn't understand how I felt, physically, and the symptoms were both elusive and excruciatingly constant. I felt on the constant verge of hallucinating. If I looked too long at a straight stretch of road, it would start to bend. Passing massive trucks, the thought of jerking the steering wheel and scraping the side of my car on their wheel wells flew into my mind, just outside the walls of my own consciousness. I started feeling like I was two people: one, the person who'd been through everything and was a reliable and solid human. And two, a maniac, every second on the verge of some terrible scream, or a swerve into traffic. I was so tired that I wasn't tired anymore. I had so much adrenaline that I couldn't ever really eat. And the feeling that I'd associated with mold followed me; it was everywhere now. In every motel, in every store, in every parking lot that I pulled over to. I pulled over at rest stops, pulled my phone out of my pocket, checked one of my environmental illness Facebook groups I'd joined to see stories of people who'd gone camping in the deepest wilderness but "cross-contaminated" themselves with their shoes. Everything felt poisonous and dangerous. I hadn't thought about my suitcase! It was the bottle of supplements that were carrying spores from Berkeley! That's why I wasn't getting better. The next motel, I left my suitcase in the car, brought only my phone and computer and wallet into the hotel room. But then, Facebook, a post: *So . . . everyone knows that Apple computer fans are notorious for toxin spread.* I closed my MacBook Air, put it in the closet. There. Was I safe now?

Now that I was alone, truly alone, couldn't really tell Winston, or anyone who loved me, about what I was doing — leaving my clothes in the car, painstakingly washing my toothbrush in hot water, hiding my computer in the closet so its invisible toxins wouldn't contaminate my cellularly remodeled airways — I had to face something I hadn't wanted to face. *I have squandered so much time,* I thought. I knew.

How many times had I looked for something to remind myself that I existed? How many times in my life had I been granted intimacy only to choose instead to be alone? How many times had someone wanted to help me and I had refused, because I had felt uncomfortable with the truth, with the uncoiling of the tightness that had for so long lived in my chest? I thought back to meetings, to people coming up to me afterward, beaming with love and light and kindness, and all I had done was snap, and speak sharply. I thought of my friend who'd asked me if I was going to be okay, at whom I'd snapped that I wasn't a psychic. I missed her. Why had I snapped at her? Why, when I'd been standing right next to someone who had just wanted to love me, had I chosen instead to walk away? It was because just as I'd believed with Allison, I'd thought that I had all the time in the world, that these little interactions didn't really matter. That there would always be another chance to do it right.

Here, alone beyond measure, all of those times that I'd managed to connect felt like gifts, like the easier, softer way, like an incredibly beautiful thing that I'd thought I'd have infinite time to develop. But why hadn't I taken advantage of how good I had felt? Why had I spent so much time creating my own suffering? Why had I refused hugs, ignored overtures? Why hadn't I written to my college roommate, who I missed? Why hadn't I apologized sooner? Why had I let entire friendships just lapse, because the friend hadn't said what I wanted her to say when I was hospitalized? Why had I let my illness *distance* me from so many people, even as it had brought me so much closer to these few?

I had to accept, while I was alone, that as much as being sick had brought me closer to so many people, it had also separated me from so many others. I had separated myself. Lying in a motel in the desert, under the star-filled sky, I had to admit to myself that I had reached a point where the facts of my life and the unknown facts of my medical situation felt impossible to explain, and so I stopped trying, and then I stopped communicating, and then, as much as I knew intellectually that I was loved, I had still built myself an island. Alone, in the desert, I wondered why I hadn't tried harder to explain things that *were* actually explicable. Maybe people *would* have understood. Why hadn't I given anyone the benefit of trying? I felt like I'd had an opportunity with regular things — surgeries, cancer scares — and now I had a weird thing and I'd blown my chances. No one would ever want to know what was happening. No one would ever believe me. I'd had the chance not to be alone, but what had I done? I'd put myself on an island and believed that no bridges could be built.

~

I spent a few nights in Colorado, but didn't feel good. And so, west. It got warmer as I crossed into Utah, started heading down in elevation from the mountain passes of Vail and Telluride. I followed signs for Moab, and then there it was, a town nestled among desert and rock monuments, once again in the middle of a landscape that loudly announced itself as being nowhere.

By this point, I'd given up on hotels. Every single one seemed to have some kind of mold infestation.

"I need a tent for one person and whatever else I need to sleep outside for a few nights," I told the guy at the downtown Moab camping store. I'd finally succumbed to direct and indirect internet advice, to fully decontaminate by sleeping in a tent. But what, I wanted to know, if the tent was moldy? *Just hope it isn't,* people said. It seemed like logic was starting to fail. If every building was to some extent moldy, wouldn't the tent factory, or the store, be moldy? If my shoes were enough to contaminate my car, what if the truck carrying the tent from the shipping container to Moab had had a moldy mattress? I thought of the networks that every object I own has to go through before it gets to me. What was the likelihood that not a single stop had been uncontaminated?

Still, it was my best chance. I bought a two-person tent that was supposed to be easy to put up, a sleeping mat, a sleeping bag, and an inflatable pillow.

I got to the campsite, laid the tent materials out, unfolded the directions, and couldn't understand them at all. *Loop ropes into stakes. Drive stakes three feet apart. Loops into hooks. Hook into loops.* I felt a burning flash of frustration shoot through my body. I wanted to throw the instructions on the ground. I wanted to throw myself on the ground. But I couldn't; this tent, this ground, they were my last chance for some kind of rest. There was a couple next to me putting their tent up. I reminded myself what it looked like to smile, how it sounded to talk.

"Can you help me?" I asked. "I have no idea what I'm doing."

"Of course!" the woman said.

I started crying. Of course there was help. Of course.

I stayed two nights in Moab. The open sky felt oppressive, and the heat was shimmering and horrible. My doctor was on vacation; I called my therapist. Hearing her voice was a tie back to the person I'd been. She'd walked me through so much, through all of the unimaginable.

"You have so many resources," she'd said to me, again and again and again.

She'd taught me how to soothe myself. But here I couldn't. I was too sick. I didn't have time.

"Can you take a pause?" she asked.

Of course I couldn't. I had to solve my problem. I had to

consider logistics. I had to figure out what to believe. Based on what I'd read on the mold avoider websites, the entire world was a threat; according to one prolific poster, the only safe place was on a mountain in Crete. I looked it up on Airbnb. I didn't tell my therapist I was looking up Cretan houses on Airbnb and seriously considering moving there forever. What the fuck was going on? No one could tell me. I couldn't even tell myself.

There was one other difference between me and everyone else I encountered.

"It's not like this is my first rodeo," I said to my therapist. I was conscious that this was happening after other, equally extraordinarily traumatic events. I felt like I'd recovered from brain and heart surgery, but here, I realized how much more time I needed to heal. There was a scratching at the back of my mind that this wasn't about mold, that this might be about trauma. What if this was my body's way of telling me that my mind couldn't cope with what had happened? What if my sensitivity to the world wasn't based in chemistry, but was instead some kind of manifestation of my inability to process what had happened? Everything had happened so fast, from thinking I was just a little tired to brain surgery to heart surgery to cancer scares to Allison's death. After years of trying to get back to my life, I had to finally accept that *this* might be my life. That I might always be a patient. That I might be a permanent citizen of the kingdom of the sick. Of course I was running away, literally and figuratively. What else was I supposed to do?

I couldn't cope. I couldn't tell anyone that I couldn't cope. I felt like the world that had expanded into a previously unknowable freedom had contracted around me and that there was no way out. I didn't know what to do. So I did the only thing I could think of. I called Lauren.

"Why don't you go back to Sedona?" she said. "At least you'll have your pals at Java Love."

～

So after all that, I drove back. Winston said he would come and be with me and we'd figure it out from there. He appreciated how hard I'd tried to find a place that would work for both of us. He was willing to give Sedona a shot.

"Your health comes first," he said, again and again.

I found a house to rent on Craigslist, for what seemed like a preposterous amount. But I'd make it work. We'd make it work. I was desperate.

"You can really pay that?" the owner asked when I came by to meet her and check it out. I must have looked like someone who couldn't get paid to do anything. I was in grubby jeans and grubby shirt, hadn't washed my hair recently, hadn't brushed it in weeks. I hadn't brought a hairbrush when I'd come on this trip, and so I'd been running my fingers through my hair after I showered, trying to manually detangle, which worked about as well as it sounds like it would.

"I have work," I said. "I get paid to write."

Not that I'd written anything, or could even imagine writing anything, but I was still getting those monthly ghostwriting payments. Thank god. That's all the landlord cared about, that I could pay the deposit immediately, which I did. The place would be available the following day, and so I had one day to get in and get settled, to try to prepare it for Winston, who was on his way from Oakland.

I felt dizzy in the house, and it was full of stuff—knick-knacks, braided tapestries and leather chairs and fabric so-fas—and, worried that decades of dust had picked up mold, I picked everything off the walls and off the tables, put everything into the garage. By myself, I hauled leather-backed chairs from the living room and down the hall, took mental snapshots (but not actual ones, I couldn't think that far in advance) of how the rooms looked, how they were decorated. I knew that I didn't feel well in the master bedroom, so I went to the back one, where I slept on the futon, poorly, waking up to feel my nose stuffed and again those mold dreams.

The next day, I waited for Winston. I got nervous. I hadn't seen him in six weeks. Did he think I'd gone into a fugue state? Was he regretting having married me? Did he believe that I was too sensitive for the world? Did he think this was trauma? How would I act? How would I say hello? I felt like I'd lived a lifetime since I'd seen him. Would he ever be able to understand? I hadn't let myself miss him, and now that he was coming I missed him so much that the thought of seeing him pierced my belly and prickled the back of my neck, and now I didn't know how to be or what to say or how to get my experiences from my head to his ear.

I heard his truck drive down the street after it got dark. I ran out. He jumped out of the car, held me, wrapped me in his arms. As soon as he was there, I could feel how alone I'd been. How desperate I'd felt. It was like getting into the warm after being in the cold but having to have been in the cold because the cold was the only place to be, and then, suddenly, after getting warm, the cold seemed, in retrospect, unsurvivable.

He came in, saw the house, looked around. We went to bed. We woke up.

"I want to make you happy," he said when we woke up together. He wrapped himself around me. I felt his forearm, the familiarity of his shoulders, the place on the back of his neck where his hair began. He was mine. He was mine again. He was a physical body and a person and he loved me and he believed in me and he was here and I didn't need to do this alone anymore and here he was. We had made it.

We stayed in Sedona for three months. That dizziness got worse, and I couldn't tolerate being inside, and so I slept in the tent on the patio for two of those months, zipping myself in every night and looking at the stars as I fell asleep. I set up my home office on the patio, felt my brain come back a little bit, typed words and sent them to architects and to my friend. Just as I'd been with my pre-brain-surgery selfies, I was public about my situation, again: I took pictures of the tent, with Bell Rock in the background, and posted them on Instagram, hoping for something — some recognition, some faith in what I was doing. Sometimes, lying in my tent at night, I tried to make myself feel the majesty of this world, looking at the glittering stars through the tears that gave me yet another scrim between this world and the next, between the world inside my head and the world everywhere else. And sometimes I felt the great expanse of our planet, our solar system, the mysteries of the infinite beyond. And sometimes I felt nothing but an aching horror and loneliness. My tent wasn't big enough for both of us. Winston was here with me, but he was inside the house. I was still lonely. I was still alone. And so my friends: Lauren came. Jason came. Another friend, Emily, came. Winston's best friend, Brad, came. I felt like all I did was drive back and forth to Phoenix airport. I'd done what had seemed like the hardest thing: I'd stopped running. And the love came to me.

I gave up on finding an answer. I committed to going day by day, symptom by symptom. I took notes for myself of what was getting better. *Hair falling out less. Sleeping okay. Not so thirsty all the time.* One morning, I walked to the very base of Bell Rock, one of the formations that I could see from our house. Too tired to go any farther, I lay on a ledge. I looked up at the sky, past the gnarled trees. I could feel all of my desperation to understand slip away. I realized that I had no choice but to accept this — this path, this life, that I was here, living in Arizona with a freaked-out husband. I realized that so much of my suffering had come from refusing to acknowledge what was happening, from believing that information would be my guide. It was the same feeling I'd had as a child, and a teen, and a young adult. The belief that if I just knew the rules I would be okay. "I surrender," I said, first under my breath. Then again, a little louder, "I surrender." I saw a bird, and another one. Objectively, I was in a beautiful place. Objectively, my body had been strong enough to take me out here. It was the subjectivity, the comparison with where I thought I should be, that hurt. "I surrender." I didn't need an answer. I just needed to breathe. To, once again, find meaning in the simplest moments. In my friends.

If it hadn't happened to me, I wouldn't believe what happened next. My doctor came back from Tahiti. I called him, told him I was sleeping in a tent in Arizona, against his advice.

"Why?" he asked. "Why? Why? Why?" he kept asking, every time I told him about sleeping in a tent, or feeling sick at the Whole Foods, or why I'd attempted Moab camping. I told him about the reactions to seemingly everything, the way that mold seemed to be everywhere, implausible as that seemed.

"There's a pattern here," he said. "I think this goes way beyond mold."

He sent me a paper on a rare disease called mast cell activation syndrome, one that tricks your body into thinking it's allergic to everything. I read the paper and cried with recognition and relief. It described years of waxing and waning symptoms, of co-appearance with allergies, and fatigue, and anemia, and many of the dramatic and less dramatic issues I had dealt with.

My reactions were physiological, real, and measurably worse. That black-and-white answer I'd been looking for? It was out there. And my experience was textbook. Symptoms would be manageable for years, according to the paper, until something turned the body on, set it all loose. Maybe it was the first time the cyst ruptured; maybe it was the trauma of all those surgeries; maybe it was that flu; maybe it was living in a very moldy house for a year. But something had profoundly affected my mast cells, which are allergic mediators and protectors of the body. My body had been, over the years, leaking histamine, cytokines, inflammatory chemicals, into my system. They made me dizzy. They made me tired. I could cope. Until I couldn't. And mold was in the picture, just not in the way I'd imagined, not with the singular focus I'd given it. Once I started tracking my reactions I realized that I *did* react to mold. And heat. And sudden weather changes. And barometric pressure shifts. And artificial flavorings. And salmon.

I'd surrendered and a day later I'd been given an answer.

My doctor started me on an incredibly convoluted protocol of antihistamines and mast cell stabilizers. I took eight pills in the morning, five with lunch, eight with dinner, and three at bedtime. He said it would take six to eight weeks for me to feel results. Sometime during the seventh week, I woke up and didn't feel that lead. I could think clearly. Strategically. I could respond to emails, could write sentences.

In other words, I felt like myself for the first time in as long as I could remember. Like a self that I had forgotten. I couldn't believe it. For so long I hadn't been able to figure out what was wrong with me, had tried to do my best, and fake it, and be okay, until finally my body had just completely rebelled, or given up, or just gotten too tired, and I had an answer. I wasn't just a stressed-out female graduate student. I wasn't a malingerer. I wasn't secretly depressed. This wasn't childhood trauma. I wanted to call every single doctor who had diagnosed me with depression or anxiety or just "having a lot on your plate right now and it's a stressful time" and force them to read this paper. The diagnosis felt like a watershed moment for me, but also for women who are sick and undiagnosed. It gave me a tool I could use anytime a doctor was dismissive, didn't listen to me. It gave me armor —there's a weird disease that people didn't know about until someone figured out how to find it, and it was also recognized by institutions such as the Mayo Clinic, and Brigham and Women's Hospital. This was not a fringe illness.

I thought back to my earlier skepticism: of myself, of others. Feeling the relief of this diagnosis allowed me to really feel how awful it had been to wrestle with constant doubt. I wish for so much to change. That (often) male doctors would believe women who come to them with difficult-to-diagnose illnesses, would move beyond assuming that they can't get out of bed because they're overwhelmed by their jobs, or childcare concerns, or grief. That doctors wouldn't say things to women that they would never say to men.

Having a diagnosis gave me an answer, however temporary. I didn't have to just be sick and never know why and sleep outside for most of my life and live in the desert forever. From everything I read, the disease was manageable, though incurable. I expected to have to manage it for the rest of my life, but I was okay with that tradeoff. For so long, I had wanted my life back. And that happened, sort of — except the life I got back wasn't the one I'd lost. It's better.

A few days after starting the medications, I started walking, at first just a little bit, in the mornings when it was coolest, and slowly, as time went on, going a little farther. As I walked, I thought about everyone I loved. I talked to Allison as I walked, for hours a day. I grew to trust the solitude, that no one would walk into me, see me talking to the sky. I also trusted the fact that Sedona is full of people literally talking to entities that no one else can see. I thought about my friends at home, about the texts they sent me, the comments they left whenever I posted a picture of Courthouse Butte, my favorite Sedona rock formation, on Instagram, the way they pretended that I was in fact posting more than basically the same picture of the same rock every few days.

I pulled myself onto ledges, put my earbuds in, and listened to the *Doctor Who* soundtrack, the one I'd danced to with Lauren. And I conjured Lauren in my mind, and then Allison, and then Winston's parents, and Jason, and everyone who'd loved me. And then I didn't need to conjure them, because they came, casually, just to visit, and it actually felt casual. Jason came for a few days, slept in the back bedroom. During the day he sat at the kitchen table and worked, and then when it got cooler, we walked to Bell Rock, to Courthouse Butte.

I asked him what he thought about what I'd done. What he'd thought about my sudden departure, my months in the desert. If he'd believed me then. If he believed me now. I felt embarrassed at how quickly I'd left Oakland, how hard I'd stuck to my mold-related guns. I was trying to disavow the self of a month before.

"I learned to trust you," he said. "From what I see, you've learned to trust yourself."

Growing up with someone knowing you along the way is painful. Embarrassing. I thought back to the earliest days of my friendship with Jason, when I'd thought he was really cool and I wanted to be cool too, versus here, where I was wearing jeans I'd bought at the Gap outlet and rompers I'd bought at Walgreens. I was very far away from the well-dressed twenty-something I'd been in New York City, where we'd met. But hadn't we all made outwardly inconceivable decisions at some point in our lives? Part of tethering myself to reality was realizing that what I'd done with my singular focus on mold—as opposed to the truth, which is that mold *is* everywhere, and it *was* significantly affecting me, but it wasn't the only cause and it wasn't the only answer—was what so many of us have done with love, or sorrow, or grief: hold on tight, as tight as we can. The way that I'd refused to let other information enter my mind, the way that I'd held fast to the truths that I thought had to be real —that the world was infested with mold, that I would never recover—was the same stubbornness I'd seen people show in relationships, or jobs. Those grooves had been so available because I'd practiced them: when I'd been unfaithful, when I'd believed that I was beyond the vagaries of human pitfalls, when I'd concerned myself with my fears of an ordinary life. I'd thought the whole time that my running from something had been so extraordinary. But it wasn't. It was the opposite. It was the most human thing in the world.

The diagnosis helped, and so did the antihistamines, but I didn't immediately get better. I realized there was a part of me that still held on to the thought that this could all be emotional, that I had been sent by some mysterious higher power to the desert, to wander and learn. That I'd needed to experience what it was like to question my perception of reality so profoundly, to spend those days and days alone, driving through the country. I remembered something a healer had told me once, that we go to the desert to die in some form, that those who find themselves drawn to the desert then return, forever changed. I hoped this would happen, and that once I surrendered I would be instantly healed, but my life was more prosaic than that. I had been desperately alone, and I had learned things about love, and then I had still felt desperately alone, and then just a little bit less alone, and then I had fully accepted, integrated into every cell in my body, that I was not alone, that I was loved, that Allison would always be with me, and still I was sick. Still my fingernails didn't grow and my hair splintered off and my coal-black under-eye circles remained. Still I was exhausted from the effort of one hour of work.

I referred to my time in the desert, even while I was there, as my nonconsensual vision quest. The nonconsensual part was easy enough to understand; I'd never intended to live here. The vision quest part was a little more elusive. I had the sense that I'd gone here for a reason, but I couldn't figure out what that reason was when I started plateauing in my recovery. Yes, I could walk, sometimes all the way around Courthouse Butte, but then I had to sleep the whole next day. And so what was I questing after? What was I supposed to be envisioning?

It was hard not to have a path. My father called me almost every day.

"Just a little better than yesterday?" he asked, every time.

I could hear the way he tried to cover up his fear and worry with optimism.

"Every day, a little better," he said, every time. I had to remind him that this isn't how my recovery was going. That there were good days and then bad days and I couldn't be sure which one would be which, so we had to live in the present now. That a good day was worth a good day not because it meant something about how the next day might feel, but because it itself was good. I thought of Allison and her relationship to hope. The way that hope lit her heart. The way that a good day, for me, was a good day.

"When do you think you'll be able to leave the desert?" people asked. I refused to answer. I didn't know. I couldn't know. And I didn't want to torture myself by planning and then having to redirect. Living in the absolute present became both a coping mechanism gifted to me by my own body, and a mode of practice that I would carry with me as long as I could.

I had always lived by ambition. I had always lived for my future. Always. What I was going to do next, how I was going to do it. When I'd first gotten sick, I'd seen every plot point as a detour, as a hairpin twist that was interfering with the way my life was *supposed* to be. I'd always been on my way somewhere. Things were going to be great when. Things would finally be okay if. All I had to do was this one thing. Invest in my future. Plan for the future. But what about now? What about this moment?

I thought of Allison again. About how what she had done with her life wasn't ever going to be visible in any kind of public record. As a child, when I didn't know if I existed for my parents, I'd dreamed of some kind of future fame. I wanted to publish so that I could know that I had mattered. But Allison hadn't published. Allison had mattered so much. I felt my life unspooling before me, and then I felt myself nudge myself back onto some path, this path. With no idea where it was going.

But was this really so different from how we all live? I thought about my friends, about their plans. One who had accidentally gotten pregnant and then realized she wanted to marry the father; my sick friend who'd planned to be a professor of government but had ended up making a movie that I knew, the minute I saw it, would change the world. Why had I thought that I would somehow be an exception to the surprises of life? I'd seen a friend mourn her father, who'd died when she was sixteen; remembered a girl freshman year who'd lost her mother when she was eight. I'd watched friends deal with difficult pregnancies, with miscarriages, with the death of their babies. At the time, I'd been so overwhelmed by not knowing what to say that I hadn't said anything at all. We all carried grief with us. We all carried the unknown.

Being able to have compassion for myself was what let me have so much more compassion for everyone else. I know it's supposed to work the other way around, that first we have compassion for others and then ourselves. But as Allison pointed out, I'm nothing if not self-centered. Realizing that my own life had taken all these twists and turns and that I was, fundamentally, sort of, sometimes, when I was feeling very enlightened, okay with them gave me an expansive place from which to reenter my friendships.

Beyond the people who kept in touch, there were also those who had missed this entire season. Who hadn't really known that I'd gotten sick, and then gotten sick again.

"I'm so bad at keeping up with you on Facebook — what's been going on?" one of my college friends said, thinking she was in for a casual catch-up about work and romantic interests. I pushed aside the feeling that her not knowing what was up with me meant I didn't matter. I wondered if I knew what was up with her. She'd bought a house near D.C. She'd mentioned something about Kilimanjaro. My uncharitable thought was that these things were so much less interesting than what I was going through. But my second thought, and I'd learned that it was my second thought that usually mattered more than my first, was that everything that we deal with is the biggest thing. That my illness and my desert quest was no more meaningful or important than my friend's doing what it took to buy a house, to climb Mount Kilimanjaro.

Part of building a bridge meant believing that everyone was suffering at capacity and experiencing joy at capacity. Maybe the plot points were different. Maybe one friend was grieving over a breakup that had ripped his soul apart; maybe another was experiencing profound joy because of a musical project that had gone well. Who was I to say that my suffering was more intense, my joy more real? I thought of Allison. How when she'd been dying of metastasized cancer and I'd been upset at Winston for not doing the dishes, she'd never told me that at least I wasn't dying of metastasized cancer. She'd taken me seriously. She'd met me wherever I was. And that's what I wanted to do for everyone else.

∾

In January of the year I left for the desert, after my brain MRI came up clear, my neurosurgeon had recommended I keep a close eye on my ovaries, and referred me to a doctor at Stanford. I had a biopsy of an ovarian cyst in February that turned out to be a dermoid; the new doctor hypothesized that the AFP tumor marker was coming from a still invisible ovarian tumor, and suggested that I get regular scans until *this* one "popped up." He was virtually certain I had some kind of low-key ovarian cancer. (It was nerve-racking how comfortable my oncologists seemed to be with the idea that we've all got little proto-cancers, that we just need to wait for them to appear.) November in Sedona marked six months since my last evaluation, and it was time for a follow-up. Fourteen phone calls and a number of complicated intrastate referrals later and I had a scan at the Phoenix Dignity Health Cancer Center, an ultrasound that revealed a very suspicious mass. My Stanford surgeon wanted to see me immediately. I had no idea if I'd be okay in the Bay Area, but the fact of a solid lesion with increased vascularity was more important than possibly being exposed to local mold.

Winston and I flew together to San Francisco. His best friend picked him up and whisked him off for dinner, and my core group of East Bay girlfriends, Megan, Marny, and Jessie, met me at baggage claim. The plan was they would drive me down to Palo Alto and spend the evening with me until Winston got back from dinner. I picked up my bag, met them in a flurry of hugs, and climbed into the back of Marny's car. Seeing their faces, feeling the dense weight of the five months that I'd felt so lost and alone, I broke into a sob. And another. And another.

I couldn't speak. Everything rushed back to me. The night in Moab when I'd thought about walking into the road, the intense loneliness I'd felt while driving from Arizona through Colorado, the adrenaline that had coursed through every millimeter of my veins to keep pushing me, to keep me alive. As much as my friends' individually coming to visit had been a soothing balm, being back, here, with friends whose eyes shone with a brightness that I recognized — this time as love — this was something different, a new phase.

We drove to our hotel. Marny got on the bed and ordered room service, slipping into a British accent halfway through her order just because it was hilarious. Jessie took a video that showed me rolling off the bed laughing. Megan stretched out on my bed, then moved when I reminded her that I needed to keep things pristine. To them, my coming back was just the next thing. But to me, it was a marker of what might be possible. I felt a little dizzy, but nothing close to how bad my reactions had been in the summer. This would be okay.

I saw my surgeon the next day.

"Let's get it out," he said of the mass.

He thought it was one of three possible types of tumors. I was scared, but I knew exactly how to prepare. We canceled the Sedona rental and flew back for one final week to pack, prepare, and host a Friendsgiving that Jason and Winston's childhood best friend, Brad, had planned for. Brad cooked a turkey; Jason sat at the kitchen table and worked on his music app. We gathered around the table and as I sat in a chair and felt my back pressed against its back, as we paused for laughter instead of a moment of silence, as we danced around the kitchen and I wore a full-body tiger suit I'd bought at Target with my friend Emily when she'd come to visit, I knew that this was enough. I'd needed to go to the desert, and my friends had followed. The four of us packed the house up in half a day, carrying the dusty furniture back from the garage, rehanging the wooden pictures I'd so frantically shoved into the storage room. Not having a lot of warning was perfect. I didn't have time to sit and wonder why I'd gone to the desert and if I was ready to go back. I had a solid mass with increased vascularity (*very* bad words in the oncology world) that we needed to get out. Once again, my body became a stronger driving force than even my mind.

Winston's parents invited us to stay with them again, this time in their bedroom as opposed to on a dining room cot. Winston's mother had come to visit us in Sedona.

"I really thought I was going to have to come do an intervention," she said, after she'd been there a day, after we'd walked around the rock.

"But I get it now; you're doing better than I've ever seen you."

I'd been desperately ill when I'd met them; as much as my love for Winston had propelled me forward, they'd only ever known me exhausted, worn out, in between surgeries and with the constant threat of a life-threatening situation. But when she saw me in the desert, post-diagnosis, post-treatment, she'd noticed a change.

"We believe you," she'd said.

We set up camp in their bedroom. And I prepared. Two days before surgery I walked the aisles of Whole Foods, collecting aloe vera juice and ginger shots and soothing teas, all things that I knew would help me feel as well as possible once the anesthesia wore off. I planned who would take me to surgery and who would take me home. Winston knew what to do. We were old hands by now, practiced at this, and practiced at being frightened of what might come next. With every other biopsy, I'd been terrified for weeks. I remembered how I'd been before brain surgery, how the terror at what might happen had been a spinning black ball, how I'd never believed that I could return to a world of caring about anything besides the sticky Velcro moments of love that made up everything good in my life.

Having survived the desert, I felt a new equilibrium. I was buoyed by memories of waking up to a piercing desert sun, to the way that I had begun to incorporate the rhythm of the stars into my mental map of the world. By the walks that Winston and I took to the Circle K some nights, chatting as we went. By the ways that he showed me the constellations he'd been tracking.

"There, that's Venus," he said sometimes, holding me close and pointing to a slightly more brightly shimmering spot in the sky. I thought maybe I would have cancer this time, and maybe it would kill me. But the worst had happened. The worst was already over.

And once again, the mass turned out to be benign.

After the surgery, Winston's parents showered me with love and understanding. His mother brought me sliced apples, pudding cups, tea. Lying in their bed, propped on pillows, my incisions slowly healing, I responded to emails and worked just as much as I'd worked the morning after brain surgery, but without the same fear and denial. I was able to absorb these blows, physical and emotional. I asked my yoga teacher to do some Skype privates with me, and there I sat in Winston's parents' bed, the laptop open, her talking me through a breath.

"Can you feel your belly rise?" she asked, and I looked, and there it was. It felt magical to me that I could think a thought like *Breathe* and my body would respond.

In the hospital the first time, I'd been given a neurological test. The doctors had taped sensors to my head, wrapped my skull in bandages. They'd hooked the sensors up to a monitor and I had watched on the screen as a blink corresponded with a flickering of activity. I licked my lips. Another flicker. I spoke. Another flicker. I lived in my body. I was my body. And my mind.

And so it was that I began to stitch myself back together. With the help of my friends.

~

After the surgery, Winston and I weren't sure what to do. After I'd been staying with his parents for a month, they gently intimated that they might like their bedroom back.

"No rush," they said. "We understand. Just, eventually."

I still felt a little uncomfortable about how much they were doing for me, but I also believed that they loved me. That they understood that none of what had happened was my fault.

I had always thought that all of this was my fault somehow.

"How did you get so sick with so many different things?" people asked, sometimes. It was a way of trying to understand randomness. If a person like me got so sick with such wildly different illnesses, what did that mean about how our world is organized? I could hear the wheels turning when people began to hear my story.

"Do you think you were born with it?" they asked.

"Is this because you grew up near nuclear radiation?" they hypothesized. (I did, actually; the Chernobyl cloud drifted over southern Germany, creating a hotspot right over the city where I'd grown up.)

"Have you ever held on to negative feelings for too long?" some of them asked. I never spoke to the third group again.

Feeling how much acceptance I received from (almost) everyone I saw rewired me on a grand scale, the way that Allison's intimate love had rewired me so many years before. The story stopped being about the time I'd gotten lost in the desert and had to beat my hands on the steering wheel to know that I was alive. The story became that I'd become reactive to some environments, gone to the desert to recuperate, and then returned. I was sick and then I got better.

I was still reactive to some places in Berkeley, but my antihistamine protocol took care of it. I took fourteen pills a day and then I took thirteen. Then twelve, then eleven, then twelve, but one was different. I slowly edged off of almost all of my medication. And I kept doing everything else, everything I could think of: desensitization, allergy testing, enzymes, iron supplements, yoga, yoga, yoga. And therapy.

~

I got sick and then I got physically better, but my mind needed time to heal. I felt a pressure to be done.

"You're better now, right?" people said, sometimes. I had to hedge.

"Mostly," I said. "I'm mostly okay."

I wanted to be totally better, to have a clean break between sick and better. But illness like this doesn't work like that. It's like having a cold that lingers, and you think every day might be the last day and tomorrow will be better and then you forget what feeling better feels like and you just hang on, and the normal changes, and you're not sure if you still have a cold or not, until one day you wake up and you just don't have a cold but you don't know what broke it or why then. And I was in the in-between, even after I got better, for over a year.

Once I was physically out of danger, my brain kicked into full gear. I had a diagnosis that made sense; no one was scanning me, and so, time and space. Time and space for everything to rush in. And it did.

I got myself another teaching position at Berkeley. Walking to meet my advisor, participating in reading groups, I felt the deep intuition that sitting with my back to the door would kill me. Sitting in a seminar and having my arm casually touched became another deep intuition: if I was touched I would die. I couldn't explain how this all felt, and I was ashamed that I couldn't outthink these intuitions.

"But you're better now. Move on," a few people said, some subtly, some overtly.

"Leave that world behind," they said, after I got a short gig writing advice columns for a wellness-related website.

My mother sent me a long email a month after Winston and I moved into an apartment in Berkeley, imploring me to move on.

"You have so many interesting thoughts about architecture and cities," she said to me. "We all want you to get back to that."

I felt relentless pressure to be done, to be finished, but my mind wouldn't let me. It told me that if I was touched again I would die. Sometimes, getting a routine blood draw,

I would have a migraine for two days afterward. The nurses at school were familiar with my chart. They were kind, and asked me about Winston, and about how things were going.

I wanted to be done and I didn't know how to be done. I was still sick sometimes. I lost days to intractable migraines that seemed tied to nothing in particular except maybe stress. I couldn't feel stress, though. I just felt that I had fallen into some kind of abyss, a different one; this one had slippery sides, and I couldn't see my way out.

A few weeks after I began teaching, I knew I couldn't do it. I called my father and my stepmother.

"I can't do this," I said.

"I think you might have . . . a touch . . . of post-traumatic stress disorder," my stepmother said. I thought since I was physically better, I couldn't possibly still be traumatized. And yet the logics that my mind told me, the intuitions I had that everyone I loved would die, that I would die if someone gave me a hug, I could understand, in moments, weren't true. I didn't want them to be true. And so I did everything I could.

I used my yoga practice. I signed up for a teacher training, and I set a rule: no one could touch me. It was enforceable because of the container of our weekends together, because there were only nine trainees total, because everyone was working through their shit. I was able to ease up during those hours, and because of that easing I was able to recognize how guarded I felt the rest of the time. And then slowly I began to touch again. First just my teacher training partner, Kristen, who was so similar to me that I felt I could trust her. And then another woman, Alice, whose brightness and raspy voice felt like a waterfall of care. I touched them and then, once I could tell my nervous system that touch wasn't only about pain, I let them touch me.

I had been touched for so many years by so many people against my will. And they were, for the most part, well-meaning touches, pats on the arm or hugs. But I had also been touched in ways that I had consented to but did not want. I had consented to every one of my surgeries, but I had also been, occasionally, roughly handled. By trainee doctors — my surgeons were all at teaching hospitals — or by nurses for whom I was just another number. I was starting to remember more, too, more about how it felt to lie down and put my head onto a plate, knowing even through the fog of Versed, the greatest anxiolytic ever produced, that my skull was about to be cracked open.

Every other weekend I went to the studio and learned the language of healing. I learned about empathic feelings, and how I picked up the sadness and the fear and the anxiety of others. "I'm not an empath," I'd written, proudly, on my application. A few weeks into the training, I realized that the opposite is true. That I am so deeply empathic that I'd had to numb myself for years with drugs and sugar and television and sex and men and women. Sometimes I don't think it's a coincidence that my illness is one of allergic reaction, of over-response to the world around me. I learned to talk my cohort through a pose, into and out of it again. I learned to touch, first just one other student, and then another, and then another. I roared in lion's breath.

One evening, I experimented with letting another student touch my head. The tremulousness of her touch sent me into panic. I opened my eyes, looked up at the familiar ceiling of the studio.

"I'm in present time, I'm in present time, I'm in present time," I whispered to myself.

I tapped my arms, willing my body to come back to present time, out of the trauma accordion, but I couldn't. It was stuck in exam rooms, surgery clinics, waiting lounges. It was stuck being touched, being scraped, being carved, being pierced. My teacher came by, sat down next to me, put her hands on my belly. I couldn't breathe.

"Get up," she said. I did. "Get into horse," she said.

I did, standing with my feet three feet apart, knees bent, my hands pressing into the tops of my thighs. And then she roared and then so did I, reaching deep into my body for a sound I had never before made. I screamed, and then the scream turned into something else, and something deep and animal and unimagined came out of my lungs, my throat. I felt the rawness of my throat, my mouth, the way in which talking to doctors and friends and Allison and Lauren and Jason and Winston had kept me alive, the way I had talked myself into existence, and I let it go.

Paying so much attention to my body for six months helped me rewire my relationship with it. I hadn't noticed how subtly a language of terror and anger had crept into my vocabulary.

"This fucking body keeps trying to kill me," I had said once, and then I said basically the same thing again and again and again. I had been so antagonistic toward my body for so long. I'd replaced any kindness toward myself I'd cultivated with an overt hostility.

"Fuck you, fucking tumor maker. What the fuck is wrong with you" was the kind of thing I thought to my body every morning, afternoon, evening.

I understood, theoretically, that this probably wasn't ideal. But I was so angry. And the only way out was through: through slowly, over the course of those weekends, beginning to learn my body again. I replaced a loathing for my pelvic cavity, with its propensity to grow weird stuff, with an appreciation for my abdominal muscles through fifteen rounds of abs. I replaced an excruciating sensitivity about my neck with an emphasis on what it felt like to stack my skull above my spine. As we learned more and more about sequencing, working with students, and understanding injuries, I learned more and more that my body could become some kind of home. Maybe one that had a couple of broken windows and weird closets, but one that was mine. I'd spent years feeling completely abstracted and then more years feeling completely dependent and trapped; here, finally, I could come back. I could come home.

And there was always Winston. After we moved back, he disappeared into a depression, finally feeling what had happened to his beloved. He had been on such high alert for years, had been prepared to lose me every second, that once he was able to believe that he wouldn't, he couldn't handle it. Of course that's how he reacted.

"He's a prince," so many people had said, watching the way he took me to the hospital, followed me to the desert. Did we all think that he and I would escape unscathed? That our marriage would not bear the scar marks of the terror we had shared? Of course we wouldn't. Of course it would. He disappeared. He felt unreachable. We hit a breaking point, one year into being back home.

And then we returned to each other. One night, the day I'd decided to give up on trying to make things better, I came home to him lying on the couch, finishing a horror movie. I sat down next to him, stroked his arm.

"Are you going to divorce me?" he asked.

"No," I said. "But I might ask you to move out."

It was the first time I didn't try to protect him from what I was feeling. My honesty opened a door we'd both tried to keep shut. And there in the dark we sat, in our new apartment, on our new couch, and we talked. We said all the things we'd been too scared to say to each other. I told him how awful I felt that I'd pulled him to the desert, that I'd gotten better and then I'd gotten so much sicker. He told me how he'd known that I was in a valley of suffering, and he hadn't wanted to burden me with his own fears, and so he'd climbed to the top of the mountain and kept a lookout for any future trouble.

"But I want you to be in the valley with me," I said.

We talked until two in the morning. We held each other, feeling the return to each other that was possible only after such distance. We were both willing to do whatever we needed to do to come back to each other. *We will,* our friends had said when we got married. And our friends did hold us. They did help us. Slowly, over the next year, we rebuilt our marriage from scratch, day by day, conversation by conversation, laugh by laugh.

Slowly, slowly, I reduced my reliance on medicine. In June of 2017, I dropped the last crumb of a medicine I'd been on to maintain my central nervous system. It was the last medication that I'd been truly tethered to, and withdrawal was brutal. But I knew how to suffer, and more important, how to trust that it would get better. Getting off of the drug was a watershed not because of the experience, but because of how I was able to deal with it. This will end, I said to myself, over and over and over again.

I got stronger and stronger. I worked on retraining my brain, on shifting the way in which it categorized that feeling that I'd come to associate with a reaction. Instead of panicking about the loss of focus, I tried to recategorize that enveloping shift. *Oh, hi, body, thank you for warning me, but we're okay!* I thought to myself, every time the shimmer started. I don't know if it's because of that, or because the antihistamines rewired my mast cells, or because my body just eventually healed, but my reactions became more and more manageable. I had always looked to information to soothe me, but getting better was a process of learning acceptance, again, just on the other side. Did I get better because I detoxed from mold? Was it *really* mast cell activation syndrome? Would I ever figure out the true underlying cause? I didn't care anymore. After years of believing that an answer, a diagnosis, would save my life, I experienced something different: a diagnosis and a treatment plan that helped, yes, but one that wasn't the centerpiece of my recovery. Surrendering was. Two years after first going to Sedona with Lauren, we returned. Being in Sedona and feeling *good* was beyond anything I'd ever imagined for myself. I'd accepted that I'd be sick forever. I'd embraced a slower life. But no. My body had other plans.

After months of recovering and slowly reentering the workforce, I got so busy with architecture-related work that I needed help with a game plan. I asked Winston's father, a businessman, for help. I drove to their house and parked the car, made a quick phone call to a client. I had made so many phone calls from a car outside their house, to doctors, insurance companies, my parents, surgeons. Never to clients. There had been so many days that I had knocked on their door, weary and hopeless and demoralized and exhausted, and they had welcomed me in, held me, hugged me, told me they would do whatever it takes. This time I bounded to their door, full of the energy that I'd remembered having in New York, after I got sober and before I got sick. His father and I talked for two and a half hours about a five-year plan.

I stunned myself with my faith that I needed to make a five-year plan. That I once again unspooled a future. I thought back to that drive in the ambulance, my dreams of a dark wood dining table, of baking a cake, of feeling just once what it was to be loved. How tiny my dreams were. How small. How specific.

I think that I truly recovered because I gave myself time. Because when I felt the pressure of the cultural narrative about recovery enter my consciousness, I heard Allison's voice telling me to rest. To be gentle with myself. Being able to set those boundaries around my body and what it did is part of what let me open them up again.

"Are you doing hugs now?" Marny asked once, before she realized that I was doing them every time.

"Yep," I said, and squeezed her. The hug was more meaningful because it hadn't always been there. And that's how it was with feeling good. With being, as I started to say finally, healthy.

∾

When I first really got sick, in February 2013, I measured my illness in weeks. Then months. Then years. It has been a little over four years since my life swerved, and I know now that the next path is coming. That soon, just as I stepped aside from what I thought I was doing and landed in the unexpected world of illness, I will soon step aside from this path and into the next one. Allison had a Post-it note on her cabinet. *We don't know what's going to happen.* And then the same note, on the cabinet right next to the first one.

"Why two of the same?" I asked her once.

"Because by the time I've finished reading it once I've forgotten it," she said.

We don't know what's going to happen. I don't know what's going to happen. But my dreams? The futures that I imagine for myself? They are both empty and full of everything. I don't know what's going to happen. But I know there will be love at every turn, that friendship will saturate my every day.

acknowledgments

Thanks to:

Adriann Ranta Zurhellen, who saw what this book could be, and Helen Atsma, whose vision and dedication brought it to life.

My teachers: Margaretta M. Lovell, Kathleen Moran, Thomas Farber, Vikram Chandra, Bharati Mukherjee, Martin Pedersen.

My doctors, especially David Turnoff, Brian Bouch, and Oliver Dorigo.

Rachel Kaplan, my most treasured interlocutor.

My friends. You are all, always and forever, in my heart.

My guides: Maddie Hanson, Elizabeth Clark.

My family, inherited and chosen.

My love, Winston Fisher.

about the author

Eva Hagberg Fisher's writing has appeared in the *New York Times, New York Times Magazine, Tin House, Wallpaper, Wired,* and *Dwell,* among other places. She is the author of two books about architecture, and holds degrees in architecture from UC Berkeley and Princeton. She is a lecturer and PhD candidate in Visual and Narrative Culture at UC Berkeley.